Samuel Hutchings

The Mode of Christian Baptism

Samuel Hutchings

The Mode of Christian Baptism

ISBN/EAN: 9783337167585

Printed in Europe, USA, Canada, Australia, Japan

Cover: Foto ©Lupo / pixelio.de

More available books at **www.hansebooks.com**

THE MODE

OF

CHRISTIAN BAPTISM

BY THE
REV. SAMUEL HUTCHINGS,
ORANGE N. J.

Apparet aspersionem quoque aquæ instar salutaris lavacri obtinere.—
CYPRIAN AD MAG.

REVISED EDITION

PHILADELPHIA
PRESBYTERIAN BOARD OF PUBLICATION
No. 1334 CHESTNUT STREET.

PREFACE.

THE mode of Baptism has been thoroughly discussed for three hundred years by the ablest Biblical scholars. To claim originality, therefore, at the present day for a work on this subject, would be presumption. All that one can now do, is to select from the facts of philology and history, availing himself of the results of modern research, place the argument in new lights, and adapt it to the wants of our time.

The present work originated in a conviction of its necessity, not so much for the purpose of changing the mode of baptism among those who insist upon immersion, as to help those who are in doubt and inquiring for the truth. The author had seen strenuous efforts made in conversation, and by loan of books, to induce converts connected with other churches to be immersed, and had known some not a little perplexed by the arguments and objections they had heard. He felt, therefore, that a book in familiar and popular style, in a spirit of candor and charity, would be useful, especially among the young.

Another and special reason for presenting this subject at this time, is its connection with the unity of the Church as prominently brought forward at the late meeting of the Evangelical Alliance. Many are longing for the removal of the barriers which men have erected to divide the disciples of Christ, and prevent their showing their oneness in him at his Memorial Supper. Even in the Baptist churches, there are many who are pained because they cannot commune with their brethren, and desire this separating wall broken down. Apart from the question of communion at the Lord's table, the discussion of the *mode* of baptism is of little consequence. If all took the course of Robert Hall, Bunyan, Spurgeon, and the English Baptists generally, who though preferring immersion yet commune with those not immersed, there would be no occasion for controversy as to the mode. But since it is contended that immersion alone is baptism, and that baptism is a pre-requisite to communion, it becomes important to show that other modes are as valid as immersion.

To relieve the dryness of dissertation, the conversational form has been adopted in this work; at the same time it has not been thought best to occupy the mind of the reader with the absorbing interest of a romance. The parties to the conversation are a pastor and two of his children on one side, and his sister and her son on the other, with a young lady whose opinions were not yet formed.

It will be seen that the author has deviated from the common method of referring first of all to the ancient Greek authors for the meaning of Baptizo. Those who make immersion the only valid baptism, claim that this was the exclusive meaning of the word in the ancient Greek classics, and rely on that as their strong argument. We go directly to the Bible. The first and main question is, not how the old heathen Greeks used the word, but how Christ and the apostles understood and used it, and how the Jews, who adopted and naturalized the word after the conquests of Alexander, used it in reference to their various ritual ablutions. It is shown in this work that there were many baptisms which could not possibly have been *immersions*, and hence that all the argument from Baptizo in classic writings weighs nothing. To gratify those however who appeal to the ancient Greeks, we have gone to their classics and Lexicons, and shown that Baptizo does not mean to dip, and is no *modal* word at all.

The author having received from several competent critics, who have examined the work in manuscript, decided approval of it, is led to believe that it will receive the approval also of those for whom it is designed. He desires to express his appreciation of the great interest taken in this work by his friend the REV. I. P. WARREN, D. D., and to acknowledge his valuable help in its final preparation for the press.

If this volume shall aid in relieving the minds of those who are perplexed, deepening in the minds of all the conviction that the spirit of Christianity is above rites and forms, and leading those who have been "baptized into Christ," to exhibit to the world their oneness in him, by partaking together at his table of the feast which commemorates his death, the author's object will be accomplished.

CONTENTS.

	Page.
CHAPTER I.	
THE EVANGELICAL ALLIANCE,	9
CHAPTER II.	
JOHN'S BAPTISM,	21
CHAPTER III.	
DIVERS BAPTISMS,	57
CHAPTER IV.	
PRACTICE AND TEACHINGS OF THE APOSTLES,	104
CHAPTER V.	
CLASSIC USAGE,	155
CHAPTER VI.	
USAGES OF THE EARLY CHURCH,	214
CHAPTER VII.	
USAGES OF THE MODERN CHURCH,	265
CHAPTER VIII.	
THE RATIONAL ARGUMENT,	294
Synoptical Index,	336

THE MODE OF BAPTISM.

CHAPTER I.

THE EVANGELICAL ALLIANCE.

"WELL," said Joseph Mason as he overtook his uncle, the Rev. Charles Stanley, and his cousin Mary, on their way home from the closing session of the World's Evangelical Alliance,—"we have had a glorious meeting. Never before have I seen any thing so nearly approaching what we hope the Millennium will be."

"It was indeed," warmly responded Mr. Stanley. "It was truly good to be there. The whole occasion has seemed to me like one of the ancient festivals of the assembled tribes of Israel."

"More than that, I think, father," said Mary. "Those, at the best, were but the gatherings of a single nation. Ours has been almost literally a *world's* meeting of devout men out of every nation under heaven. And then it was good to see so many evangelical denominations joining in it. I am sure no person present could help feeling something of the blessedness of Christian unity, — that which our Lord prayed for so fervently in behalf of his dear people, 'that they all may be one, as thou, Father, art in me and I in thee, that the world may believe that thou hast sent me.'"

"And if there were any who did not feel its sweetness, they must still have felt its power," remarked her father. "I have often thought of the significance of those last words. 'That the world may believe.'"

"Yes," rejoined Joseph, "nothing can be a more convincing demonstration of the truth of Christianity than its power to fuse into one the hearts of men of different nationalities, languages, education, and beliefs on all other subjects: and nothing more affecting than to see the manifestation of that unity in the prayers, and testimonies of personal experience, and songs of praise, which we have witnessed during this great religious Jubilee."

"There was one thing wanting, I think," said Mary, "to complete that expression. We ought to have had at least one united communion season at the table of the Lord. Never was there a more fitting occasion, or one when it would have been more delightful to the communicants or more impressive to the world."

"But that, you know, cousin Mary, would have been hardly practicable," replied Joseph.

"And why not?" she asked.

"Oh — well — you know that there were those whose principles would not have permitted them to join in it."

"More shame to their principles, then, I think!" she exclaimed with some warmth. Then suddenly recollecting herself, she added, "Oh, I forgot, Joseph, your close communion sentiments. I did not mean to hurt your feelings. And yet, really, I don't see how you can cling to them at such a time as this."

"You have not hurt my feelings," he replied, "because I know that you did not intend to do so. And indeed I will own to you that the necessity of declining such an act of Christian fellowship on such an occasion is a painful one. I am longing for the day to come when we can all say truly, not only 'one Lord and one faith,' but also, 'one *baptism;*' and then will follow in natural and beautiful sequence, one communion table."

The young man said this in a tone of deep seriousness and even tenderness, which showed that his heart was touched, and their arrival at the house of his mother in ———th Street, interrupted the conversation.

"Come in," said he, as he passed up the steps; "it is not late; mother will be glad to see you."

They entered, and were received with a hearty greeting. Mrs. Mason was a sister of Mr. Stanley's. His wife had died some years before, leaving two children, Arthur and Mary, both young, and this aunt had cherished for them, in their bereavement, almost the same tenderness as for her own. Her health was now delicate, and she had not felt strong enough to attend the meetings of the Alliance, but she had heard reports of them from her son, and rejoiced greatly in the excellent spirit manifested in them, and the promise they gave of good to the cause of religion.

Joseph Mason was a young man of fine talents and liberal education. He had recently commenced the practice of law, and bade fair in a few years to rise to eminence in it. He was still a bachelor, residing with his mother, though expecting ere long to marry a young lady every way worthy of his choice. His cousin, Arthur Stanley, was a little younger than himself, and was now engaged in the study of medicine. Both of them were active members of the Young Men's Christian Association, whose guests the Alliance had been during its sessions. Young Mason had professed religion in the Baptist church, to which, also, his parents belonged, while Arthur and his sister were members of the Presbyterian Church, under the pastoral care of their father.

After a little general conversation upon the meeting of the evening, Mary turned again to Joseph and said,

"But do you feel, cousin, that you could not commune at the Lord's table with such men as were gathered in this Alliance? There was the chairman, President Woolsey, a man combining the highest graces of piety with the profoundest scholarship, and Dr. Adams, the venerable pastor, learned, scholarly and devout, and the excellent Bishop —— of the Methodist Church. And from beyond the sea, the Dean of Canterbury, and the eloquent Dr. Parker, and Prof. Christlieb, — oh! I can't tell them all, — the very best men in the world. You can't commune with them! And is it all because they have not been baptized in just the way you have been?"

"No, cousin Mary, it is not that. If it were merely a difference in the *form* of baptism I could not make so much of it. It is rather because *they have not been baptized at all.* We cannot admit that sprinkling a little water upon a person is, in any sense, a Christian baptism."

"And I suppose, inasmuch as baptism is the door of the church," said Mr. Stanley, "that you would go on and pronounce these, and all others who like them have not been immersed, as not within the church at all."

"Yes, sir; we are compelled to accept that inference."

"And I take it this is the view commonly held by our Baptist friends. I fell in not long ago with an article by Dr. S. F. Smith, one of the prominent ministers and hymn-writers of the denomination, which for its outspoken plainness in avowing such sentiments I preserved as a curiosity of the nineteenth century. It appeared under his own name in the Watchman and Reflector of Aug. 1, 1872. I will read only the first and last paragraphs. The article is entitled, 'Is the Baptist Church a Schism?'

"'We maintain,' says he, 'that the Baptist church is the church of Christ and the *only* church of Christ on earth.' (I emphasize his own Italics.) 'It is not a schism, but every other body professing to be a church is a schism. You may think this is uncharitable, but I believe logic and experience and the investigation of the Divine-word will convince you.' Then after giving a specimen of his 'logic' in which, as usual with Baptists, one of the premises is a simple assumption that the Greek word *baptizo* means immersion and nothing else, he derives his conclusion thus: 'From these principles it follows, that the Baptist church is Christ's church as originally existing, and *all other so called churches are only schisms*. There is but one main trunk; all else are *slabs* split off from it.'"

"Shocking!" cried Mary. "Is it possible that any enlightened Christian man can, at this day, take such extreme ground as this? Why, .

nothing but the most explicit and certain declarations of the Scriptures could warrant it."

"You may well say that," continued her father. "A position so exclusive, so destructive of the unity of the church of Christ, and so well calculated to wound the feelings of others confessedly no way inferior in all Christian graces and attainments, ought to rest on the most indisputable grounds. Such a position unchurches by far the largest portion of Christendom. No matter how many evidences they give of being true Christians, in vital union with the Lord himself; no matter how abundant the fruits of their piety, in faith and holy living and devotion to his cause on earth; no matter how richly they may enjoy the baptism of the Holy Ghost, making them like Christ in zeal and love and steadfastness, still if they have not been baptized, not only in what they sincerely believe to be a proper manner, but by being *dipped under water*, they are not within the church of Christ, and have no covenanted title to its privileges and blessings! And we well know that with these views their practice, for the most part, coincides. They treat other Christians as unbaptized persons; they will not commune with them at the table of the Lord;

they will not receive them without re-baptism to their own churches, nor join with them in translating and circulating the Bible among the heathen. And, observe, this judgment of their fellow Christians, this saber-stroke, which, with a single swoop cuts through the one living body of Christ's followers, is not made on account of a difference in doctrine or practice, apart from the rite in question, not on the pretense of anything fundamental to Christian experience or usefulness, but solely on the point whether a *rite* which is only the outer symbol of a truth,—the 'shadow of a shade,' as one has well expressed it,—shall be performed in one way or another!"

Mr. Stanley spoke with some emphasis, as his age and character warranted him in doing. Joseph replied:

"But if our views are right, uncle, as to what baptism *is*, we cannot be held responsible for the consequences which flow from them. The responsibility for whatever discord or schism may result, must rest with those who differ from us."

"I agree with you in saying that conclusions cannot be separated from their premises," replied Mr. Stanley; "and so, on the other hand, premises may be fairly tested by their conclusions. If you can show a jury by fair argument that your opponent's claim leads inevitably to results which their common sense and manly feelings disown, you have no fear for the verdict they will render."

"But the principles on which we stand are precisely the same that are recognized by other denominations," urged Joseph. "The whole question is narrowed down to this: Is an unimmersed person baptized? You yourself do not admit unbaptized persons to your communion table; why, then, are you not as strict close communionists as ourselves?"

"The two cases are not at all parallel. With us, 'an unbaptized person' does not mean one acknowledged to be a sincere Christian, who believes in baptism, and has, according to his own sincere and best judgment, been baptized, though in a different way from ourselves, but one who does not pretend to have rendered obedience to Christ's commands, or in some way gives evidence that he is not a truly regenerated soul. We exclude him, *not* because he has not been baptized, but presumptively because he has not been converted."

"Well," said Joseph, "it comes to very nearly

the same thing. Christ commands men to be baptized, that is, immersed, and he who, knowing this, refuses or neglects to do so, disobeys Christ. I will not say he is not a Christian; it is not for us to judge his heart; but we do say he does not give us that evidence of it which, according to the Bible, warrants his reception to the table of the Lord. 'Ye are my friends,' said Christ himself, 'if ye do *whatsoever* I command you.'"

"Your reasoning fails in a very vital point. You say 'baptized, that is immersed,' which quietly *assumes* the very matter in dispute. Now it can be shown from the Bible, I think, that no exclusive mode is required for valid baptism, or if there be, it is sprinkling, not immersion."

"I wish you would show it to us, father," said Mary. "I, for one, have never investigated the matter thoroughly, yet the truth is as important to me, and to Arthur, as it is to Aunt Emily and Joseph. If we *are* unbaptized persons, and out of the true church of Christ, I want to know it. Will you let us form a class for the study of the subject, under your tuition?"

"Of course, I will not refuse, if you request it, though to tell the truth, I have little taste for these questions which separate evangelical Christians. But whom do you mean by 'us?' Cousin Joseph is doubtless thoroughly posted on the subject already."

"No, sir; I should not like to be left out if such a class were formed. It would give me great pleasure to go over the subject with you, and I doubt not you can give me much instruction concerning it. I would only like to stipulate, for mother's sake, who cannot go out, that if the class be formed it shall meet here, unless indeed, it would be inconvenient to you."

Mrs. Mason objected to having the arrangements shaped with any special reference to her; but as the party all protested they should prefer to meet there rather than any where else, she gave her assent.

"When shall it be, then?" asked Mr. Stanley.

"Oh, as soon as possible!" cried the impulsive Mary. "I vote for to-morrow evening."

"Very well, then," said Joseph, "to-morrow evening let it be."

CHAPTER II.

JOHN'S BAPTISM.

ON the next evening, the party assembled as they had agreed, in the cosy sitting-room of Mrs. Mason, Arthur Stanley accompanying his father and sister. A Bible and a Concordance lay upon the center table, and several smaller Bibles were distributed about it. In the library, occupying a recess of the room, was Webster's large Dictionary, and Joseph had placed there a Greek Testament and Lexicon, with several other books furnished him by his pastor, the Rev. Dr. ——, whom he had privately consulted in respect to the approaching interview.

The cousins were all in the best of spirits, anticipating the delight which bright and ingenuous minds ever feel in the search after truth, with the added interest of its being a subject appealing directly to their tenderest religious feelings. Mrs. Mason herself showed a faint tinge of pleasurable excitement in her pale cheek, as she returned the caresses of her niece, and found her usually quiet apartment a scene of so much interest. Beside her was a young lady of about Mary's age, whom the latter seized by the hand with the warmest expressions of pleasure.

"Why, Nellie Ashton, I am delighted to see you. You will join us in our study, won't you? I was saying to Arthur that I hoped Joseph would bring Nellie in too. Cousin Joe, we are very much obliged to you."

Miss Ashton was the fiancée of Joseph Mason, a quiet and somewhat reserved young lady, but with a fine understanding and a warm and generous heart. She had quite recently obtained a Christian hope, though she had not as yet made a profession of religion. This was now beginning to press itself upon her consideration as a matter of personal duty. In one respect it tried her greatly. With her anticipation of a life-long union with Joseph, she could not bear to be separated from him in the fellowship of the church, and with her devoted attachment to her parents she could as little endure the thought of separating herself from them by joining a close communion church. Her lover had been too delicate to press his views upon her, and yet she knew well his wishes, while her mother, though anxious that Nellie should satisfy her own conscience, was even more than herself pained that such a life barrier should be erected between them, and, as she regarded it, for no sufficient reason. It was, then, quite opportunely, as Joseph felt, that this discussion on the mode of baptism, was suggested by his lively cousin; for though he knew and greatly respected his uncle's learning and abilities, yet so certain did he feel of the strength of his cause, and withal his own powers of persuasion with such an auditor, that he had no doubt of the result, without subjecting himself to the imputation of making her regard for him an instrument for proselyting her to his faith.

Placing Mr. Stanley at the head of the table, and Mrs. Mason in a large easy chair by his side, the party arranged themselves around it, and Mary, ever foremost in suggestion, cried merrily:

"Well, here we are, all ready. Now, how shall we begin?"

"I think," said Mr. Stanley, "that we should

turn to the *institution* of baptism by our Lord. Here it is, in Matt. 28 : 19. 'Go ye therefore and teach all nations, BAPTIZING THEM IN THE NAME OF THE FATHER, AND OF THE SON, AND OF THE HOLY GHOST.' Our business, as it seems to me, is simply to ascertain the import of this divine command."

"And in order to do this, we must take the Greek word *baptizo*, and see what its meaning was among the native Greeks," said Joseph, who had received some hints from his pastor as to the most advisable method of procedure. "If we would ascertain the exact import of a word, we should inquire of those who spoke it as a part of their vernacular tongue."

"Perhaps so," replied Mr. Stanley, "but is it not more to the point to find out what our Lord himself meant? That is our object, is it not?"

"Certainly," said Joseph; "but it comes to the same thing. The commission was given in Greek, and of course is to be understood according to the ordinary usage of the Greek speaking people."

"I am not so sure as to that," replied Mr. Stanley. "The Greeks were heathen, you know, and used the language to express their own heathen ideas. We want to know, not what these were or might have been, but what Christ's idea was. And this we should ascertain in the same way that we would seek the meaning of any other ancient document."

"How is that?" inquired Arthur.

"I will illustrate it by an example. Sir William Blackstone, in his 'Commentaries on the Laws of England,' says that a law of King Edward III. forbade 'all Ecclesiastical persons to purchase *provisions* at Rome.' This seems to us a very singular law, and might well lead one to stop and ask what it could mean. Now, suppose a controversy should arise as to the signification of the word 'provisions.' It would avail nothing to show that its usual meaning is food, or victuals, or to search the dictionaries and find the etymology, or to ascertain how the historians and poets and philosophers of past times had used it. We should rather inquire under what circumstances the law was made; what were its occasion and object; how the king's ministers and courtiers understood it; what was done in executing it, etc. 'The law,' said Blackstone, 'might seem to prohibit the buying of grain, and other *victuals;* but when we consider that the statute was made to repress the usurpations of the Papal See; and that nominations to benefices by the Pope were called "provisions," we shall see that the restraint is intended to be laid on such provisions only.' So in the present case, our simple task is to inquire *what Christ meant*, in giving his commands. For what he meant is the law, whether he used words as the heathen Greeks did or not."

"I think that is very reasonable, so far as I understand it," said Mrs. Mason. "I'm sure what *I* want to know is what my Saviour meant, when he commanded me to be baptized. If I can find out this, it matters little what others mean."

"What then," said Arthur, "should be our first inquiry in this case?"

"Obviously, how the *apostles* to whom he gave the commission understood him."

"And how shall we do this?" said Mary.

"By asking what *means* they had of understanding him; what was their *practice* in carrying out his command; and what were their own *teachings and instructions* concerning it."

"And first what *means* had they for understanding our Lord? He commanded, 'Go and baptize.' What did they know of baptism? Had they ever seen or heard of it before?"

"Oh yes," said Mary, "two of them at least, perhaps more, had been disciples of John the Baptist (John 1: 35); and Christ himself had been baptized by him. Of course, all of them must have been familiar with John's baptism."

"Very good," said Joseph. "And this brings us directly to John's baptism as the inspired pattern of the ordinance; and this we know was by immersion."

"But, father," objected Mary, "John's baptism was not *Christian* baptism, was it? I thought it was a mere preparatory rite belonging to the old dispensation, and no part of Christianity proper."

"No matter, now," said her father. "We may go to it to find out what was the *thing* to be done, whether it was to be done for the same purpose or not. Arthur amputates a leg, to study its anatomy. Suppose his Professor should send him to amputate the leg of a living person. The object would be different, the circumstances and results would all be different, still he might refer to the former to show what the doctor meant in giving the order."

"Well then," said Mary, laughing, "let us for once 'go down to Jordan,' as Aunt Emily so often says, and see what was done there. Nellie, will you please read us the account."

"Which shall I read?" said the latter. It is found, I believe, in each of the four Gospels."

"It does not matter which," said Mr. Stanley.

Miss Ashton read the account in the third chapter of Matthew. As she finished, Joseph remarked,

"There, you perceive how it was—'And were baptized of him *in* Jordan.' Manifestly by immersion in the river."

"We shall see as to that presently," said Mr. Stanley. "Let me call your attention to another thing first, *the great multitudes who came for this purpose.* Please read that verse again, Miss Nellie."

She read: "Then went out to him Jerusalem, and all Judæa, and all the region round about Jordan."

"Now," continued the pastor, "Jerusalem was at this time in its palmiest days, having been re-built, enlarged and beautified by Herod the Great. Think of its vast population; think of the innumerable cities and villages of Palestine, the ruins of which meet the traveler even now, on almost every square mile of its territory.

Remember what mighty armies were raised here for its protection; recall the fact that at the siege of Jerusalem alone, which occurred only about forty years later, Josephus says one million, one hundred thousand Jews perished. There was a part of Peræa beside, east of the river — for the language is 'all the region *round about* Jordan.' I do not know what the aggregate number of such a population was, but it must have been very great, — several millions, at least. And I was thinking if John had to immerse them all one by one in the river, what a task the poor man had!"

"But you do not suppose, Mr. Stanley, that every man, woman, and child of that great population were baptized, do you?" asked Nellie.

"No, I presume not. We are to take the statement in a common sense way. The sick, the aged, the crippled, etc., must be excepted. So, for various reasons, must many others. Indeed, I would be willing to take the expression as a general one, meaning simply the greater part of the people, or more simply still a very great number, but even so the difficulty remains; John could not have performed the task."

"It has been suggested," said Arthur, "that it

is not meant that all the *people* of those places went to him, but some from *all places ;* so that all had, so to speak, a representation there."

" But Mark," replied Mary, " says it was ' *they* of Jerusalem,' that is the people, and ' they were *all* baptized of him.' Luke says also that ' all the people were baptized,' and that they were 'a multitude.' "

" Well, not to press the matter too closely, it is evident that there was a very great number. Robert Hall, the eminent English Baptist, admits that it was ' a prodigious multitude.' (vol. 1: page 361.) Suppose we call it half a million. John's ministry, before Herod put him in prison, lasted not more than eighteen months; probably less. Now to have immersed so many in that time would have been more than two every minute, for eight hours a day, for that whole period — which I venture to pronounce a simple impossibility. No man could have strength to do it; and besides, just think of him as standing waist deep in the river eight hours a day for eighteen months together ! "

" But," replied Joseph, " you are not sure he did stand *in* the water. He may have stood upon the shore, while he immersed the people."

JOHN'S BAPTISM.

"That is a mere guess, which, after all, will not relieve the difficulty. The task so performed would have been so much the harder. It might have been easy enough to thrust them in, but to lift them out again would have been another thing. Let us try to take a common sense view of the matter, if possible."

"But Robert Hall thinks that John did not perform the work alone," said Joseph. "He may have had assistants. Jesus also baptized, but he did it *through* his disciples." John 4: 2.

"Which conjecture is only a confession that otherwise it could not have been done."

"Besides," added Arthur, "that fact respecting Christ is expressly told us, while nothing of the sort is said of John. It is positively said, they were *all baptized by him*." Mark 1: 5.

"True," replied his father. "And we ought not to resort to guesses when we undertake to unchurch all others for not agreeing with us. Looking now at the thing all round, in a plain, common sense way, I cannot resist the conclusion that the baptism by John of all those multitudes by immersion was just an impossibility. That, then, is one thing about baptism which I regard as *settled*. It could not have been done without a miracle."

"Yet we read that John did no miracle," quietly observed Nellie.

"That is true, Miss Ashton; but for him to have endured such a labor and such a *soaking* for eighteen months together, and have escaped alive, would have been a stupendous miracle."

"Then there is the question of the clothes," suggested Arthur.

"What is that?" asked Mary.

"Why, the garments they were baptized in. Where do you suppose they obtained a sufficient supply of baptismal robes, Aunt Emily?"

"Oh, it was a warm climate, you know, and they would not have needed much clothing," replied Mrs. Mason.

"But they would have wanted some," persisted Mary. "We cannot suppose them to have gone into the river, with their ordinary clothes on, and then sat in the sun on the bank to dry. Neither did they bring changes of garments with them for that purpose."

"In whatever light you look at it," said Mr. Stanley, "you see the difficulty. I know of no way in which it can be avoided or diminished. To my own mind it seems sufficient to decide the whole question. Here, at the outset, in the very origin and pattern, as many deem it, of our Christian rite we have a baptism, administered to vast multitudes of people, among them to our Lord himself, which, upon any rational view of it, could not have been done by immersion."

"Why, then," asked Nellie, "if John did not immerse these multitudes, did he go to the Jordan to baptize?"

"If I remember rightly, it is nowhere said that he did go there for that purpose. He was *in* the wilderness, where he had always lived; that was his home you know, (Luke 1: 80). The people came there to hear him preach, and *being there*, in the vicinity of the Jordan, it was most convenient for him to baptize those who professed penitence, in or at that river. Baptism was always performed where the person to be baptized happened to be, in the house, in the prison, at a fountain by the roadside, or at a neighboring stream."

"It seems to me," observed Arthur, "that in judging of events occurring in other times and countries, we are apt to be misled by inferences from circumstances or habits with which we are familiar. To read of a baptism now administered in or at a river or lake would convey the idea that it was performed by immersion, because water is every where so abundant, and the facilities for administration so great, that we naturally infer that none would take the trouble to go to such a place but for that special purpose."

" Your observation, my son, is quite just. I have no doubt that this unconscious inference in multitudes of cases is what determines the whole question. ' John baptized in Jordan,' they say; '*therefore* he immersed; *therefore* immersion only is baptism.' "

" But what else could have caused him to resort to the river?" asked Nellie.

" You forget that such vast numbers of people, many of them coming from a considerable distance, with their asses and camels, which were used for riding and carrying tents and other equipage, would have required large supplies even for drinking. They would need also water for cooking, and performing the numerous ablutions prescribed by their ceremonial law. ' For the Pharisees, and all the Jews, except they wash their hands oft, eat not.' (Mark 7: 3). The country though not strictly a desert was very sparsely settled, and there were but few wells or cisterns which could afford it, and during a large part of the year the fountains and rivulets were wholly dry."

"Yes," said Mary, "and you know Nellie, that even in this country, where we have water enough every where, one of the first things thought of in selecting a place for a military encampment, a cattle show, a camp meeting, or any large gathering of the people, is to find a spot near some stream or lake that shall afford a plentiful supply of this indispensable article. So you see as clear as day — at least I do, — that the fact that John resorted to the Jordan as the scene of his labors, is no proof that he performed his baptisms solely or at all by immersion."

"But it is expressly said that they went down *into* the river," urged Joseph.

"Is it?" replied Mr. Stanley. "I was not aware of the fact. Do you find such a statement any where, Miss Nellie?"

"No, I think not," answered the latter, after some little looking.

"Well, at any rate, it is said that he baptized *in* Jordan, and that implies that he *went* in," said Joseph.

"Not quite," returned his uncle, smiling. "I saw a few days since, some Dutch women washing clothes in the Hudson, but they had not gone *into* the stream for that purpose. Besides, it is said that 'John did baptize *in* the wilderness.' Does this imply that he thrust persons beneath the sand and dust of the desert?"

"It is said that Christ, after his baptism, went up straightway *out of* the water," remarked Miss Ashton. Matt. 3: 16.

"True, but it would have been more correct to have read *from*. The Greek preposition employed here, is not the same that is used in the case of the eunuch. Prof. Stuart, whose critical judgment on such a point cannot be questioned, says, 'I have found no example where it — *apo* — is applied to indicate a movement out of a liquid into the air. To designate *emerging from* any thing that is liquid, I have never found it applied.' (Bib. Rep. vol. 3; page 320). Further the verb, *anabaino*, will not admit that signification. It means to *go up, to ascend*, as in ascending the bank of a river. 'As to emerging from the water,' says Stuart, 'I can find no such meaning attached to it.'"

"After all, I am not inclined to insist on these minute points of construction. The Greek prepositions, *eis, en, apo*, and *ek*, as every Greek scholar knows, are quite flexible in their use, a great deal depending upon the connection and construction of the sentences in which they stand. Of themselves, they are not a sufficient ground to rest any important doctrine upon, much less one involving the unity of the church of Christ. For one, I have no objection to concede that John and those who were to be baptized did go *into* the river, and that the baptism was performed *in* the river. But this is far from saying that they were immersed. In that country and climate, with the prevailing habits of dress, one of the easiest ways of getting access to the water would be to step with the unsandaled feet into the margin of the stream. But neither this, nor the subsequent return was any part of the baptism. Standing thus in the water, ankle- or possibly knee-deep, the liquid was taken up in the hand or a dish, and poured or sprinkled upon the head of the recipient. That this was the view of the matter held in the early Christian Church, is apparent from the representations of Christ's baptism given in ancient pictures and sculptures. (See pp. 252 to 259). Or what is more probable, in the baptism of these great multitudes, they were arranged along the shore, and sprinkled by John with a bunch of hyssop, or something similar, as Moses sprinkled the vast congregation of Israel at the foot of Mt. Sinai. Heb. 9: 19."

"Oh, I never thought of that event in this connection!" exclaimed Mary. "But that was not a baptism, was it?"

"No, not Christian baptism, but it was nevertheless *a* baptism, and is distinctly referred to by that name, with many other Jewish washings, in the Epistle to the Hebrews. But letting that pass for the present, you see how such an act could be done easily and appropriately. The number of the Israelites exceeded two millions, yet it is expressly said that Moses sprinkled them all. Heb. 9: 19."

"I see it, I see it!" exclaimed Mary, with enthusiasm. "It is perfectly clear to me now. Don't you think so, Auntie?"

"Yes, my dear, I have no doubt it is perfectly clear *to you*, as you say, and indeed your father has succeeded in putting the matter in a plausible light, I confess. But I cannot share all your enthusiasm, and I am too old a Baptist to be persuaded that John the Baptist, of all men, baptized the people that came to him by *sprinkling!*"

JOHN'S BAPTISM. 39

"Not only do I think so, Aunt Emily," said Mr. Stanley, "but I suspect if we should examine carefully we should find that the very rite which John was now administering in the Jordan, the 'baptism of repentance,' as it was called, if traced back to its original source *required* sprinkling."

"You surprise me greatly, sir," said Joseph, "by such a statement. What, pray, do you regard as the source of that rite?"

"You will have observed that there are no indications that either John or the people regarded it as anything new, at least in form. They made no inquiries about it, as they would if not already familiar with it. Neither did the call to repentance which he was commissioned to address to the nation, differ essentially, in its nature, from similar messages which had been sent to them through the earlier prophets. The occasion indeed was new, the near approach of 'the kingdom of heaven' and the necessity of preparing for it. But repentance was the same thing it had ever been, and the symbol of forgiveness and cleansing one with which the nation had long been familiar. David, a thousand years before, had cried out in contrition of spirit, 'Wash me thoroughly from mine iniquity and cleanse me from my sin. For I acknowledge my transgressions, and my sin is ever before me. Purge me with hyssop, and I shall be clean, wash me, and I shall be whiter than snow. (Ps. 51 : 3, 7.) And Isaiah, 'Wash ye ; make you clean ; put away the evil of your doings from before mine eyes ; cease to do evil ; learn to do well.' (1 : 16, 27). And Jeremiah, 'For though thou wash thee with niter, and take thee much soap, yet thine iniquity is marked before me," saith the Lord God. (2 ; 22.)

"Now these rites of washing and cleansing were prescribed in the ancient law. They were of various kinds, by blood, by oil, and by water, or water mixed with ashes, and in all cases when administered to *persons* they were to be performed by anointing, pouring, or sprinkling — the latter often with a bunch of hyssop — but NEVER BY IMMERSION. And this fact had become so familiar to the nation that all their thoughts and utterances respecting penitence and forgiveness and cleansing spontaneously shaped themselves in this mold. It became, in their view, the natural way to express them. When, therefore, John appeared preaching repentance, he would of course, apart from any special suggestions of the prophetic Spirit, fix on this ancient mode of purification, divinely appointed, practiced by the nation for fifteen hundred years, and inwrought into all the devoutest utterances of the most holy men. And how readily would the nation thus trained recognize its import and its propriety, and receive it, when satisfied of the authenticity of his mission, as the legitimate expression of penitence and purification, never wondering at it, needing no explanation of it, but even seeing in it a new evidence that God had still respect to the rites he had appointed, and the law which, for fifteen centuries, had been a covenant between him and his people."

"But do I understand you to say," asked Nellie, "that these purifying rites were never performed by immersion? Were not persons often commanded to wash their clothes and bathe themselves in water?"

"I mean that the officiating *priest* was never commanded to immerse anybody, or any thing. Possibly I should make an exception in case of articles taken as spoil in time of war, (Num. 31: 23); though it is not said that this should be done by the priest. As to the general word 'wash' we all know that it does not necessarily mean immersion.[1] Many persons now wash themselves all over, every day, yet few do it, I think, in a plunge bath. Individuals, either before or after the official act of the priest, washed their clothes and their persons, privately, as decency required, and this they may have done by dipping, or rinsing, or pouring, or scrubbing, or any other convenient way. *If* they immersed themselves, which unless in the near proximity of a river or public pool, was probably not often done, as we have no account of private baths sufficient for the purpose, it was because of the convenience or the luxury, and not because it was required. The only washing enjoined upon or ever performed by an official administrator, was done by *sprinkling or pouring*. I believe, therefore, that John must have performed his baptism in the same way. With such a memorable and illustrious example before him, of cleansing great multitudes of persons by sprinkling, as that performed by Moses at the foot of Mt. Sinai, I can-

---

[1] "We find no example among all the Levitical washings or ablutions where immersion of the person is required. The word *rachatz* which is almost uniformly employed, and which our translators have rendered wash and bathe, does not imply immersion." Prof. Stuart, in Bib. Rep. vol. 3: page 341.

not conceive why John should have ever thought of any other way, nor do I see how any other was possible."

"You have constructed a very plausible theory, Uncle, I admit," said Joseph. "But if John's baptism was simply one of the ancient rites of purification, why was it not sometimes called purification?"

"It was, I think," replied Mr. Stanley. "Please turn to John 3 : 25, and read to us, Miss Nellie."

She did so. "Then there arose a question between some of John's disciples and the Jews[1] about purifying."

"Oh, I never knew what that meant," said Mary. "Had it anything to do with this subject?"

"We shall see," said her father. "Precisely the nature of the dispute is not stated, but it was clearly something growing out of the two baptisms which Jesus and John were then administering. Perhaps John's disciples were jealous of the growing popularity of this new teacher n securing a greater number of converts than their master, who a little while before had had

---

The best critical authorities read "a Jew."

all Palestine running after him. Whatever the trouble was, it was something growing out of this matter of baptism, and this the Evangelist calls a 'question about *purifying*.' Plainly, then, it was regarded as one of the purificatory washings with which they were so familiar. It does not seem to have awakened any question as to its form, as it certainly would have done from those who were such sticklers for prescribed forms, had it differed in any respect from ancient and recognized usage."

"I think," said Nellie, "that the Pharisees had at first denied, or at least questioned, John's authority to baptize, had they not?"

"Yes," replied Mr. Stanley, "and that reminds me that this is another of the facts which strongly confirm the view I have taken of its nature and form. Have you the passage before you?"

"Yes, it is in John 1: 19-27."

"It had been predicted," said Mr. Stanley, "that the Messiah would come as a *Purifier*. 'Who,' exclaimed Malachi, (3: 2) 'may abide the day of his coming, and who shall stand when he appeareth? For he is like a refiner's fire and like fuller's soap; and he shall sit as a refiner and purifier of silver, and he shall *purify* the sons of Levi, and purge them as gold and silver, that they may offer unto the Lord an offering in righteousness.' This was the very latest utterance of the prophets concerning the promised 'hope of Israel,' and one on which the eye of the nation must have specially rested during all the time preceding its fulfillment. When John, therefore, came calling the people to repentance, and administering the well known rite of purification, it was natural for the Pharisees to inquire whether he claimed to be the Messiah, the expected Purifier. Upon his replying in the negative, they asked, 'Why *baptizest* thou then?' That is, if you are not the Purifier that has been promised us, why do you purify? They recognized the nature and form of the rite, but could not understand why he should undertake to administer it in such a conspicuous and extraordinary manner, unless he claimed also to be the Messiah, whose special prerogative it was to be."

"All this seems very plain," remarked Arthur, "and I don't see what can be said against it. I confess I always had a sort of feeling that this baptism of John was one of the Baptists' strongest arguments in favor of their views, but I begin to think it is one of the strongest against them."

"I think so, too," replied his father. "And there is one thing more which completes and crowns the argument, and that is the close connection and parallelism between it and the baptism of the Holy Spirit."

"But the baptism of the Spirit was not a literal baptism at all," replied Joseph. "It was only *figuratively* such, so called because of its copiousness, which, as it were, immersed one in an ocean of divine grace. All our ministers agree that it was a figurative immersion." Carson, page 87.

"Oh, cousin, you surely are not in earnest!" exclaimed Mary. "Immersion in the Holy Ghost! What a shocking, I had almost said, what a blasphemous idea!"

"I am aware that such is the Baptist view of the matter," said her father. "However, we will not dispute as to that now; we shall have another occasion to consider it by-and-by. But certainly the form divinely chosen to *exhibit* that baptism to men was not that of immersion, but of outpouring. John's baptism symbolized this, as the less symbolizes the greater. How natural, not to say how essential to an emblem that it should *resemble* that which it represents! Such was the case with all the types and shadows of the ceremonial law; so far as material things could resemble spiritual things, they were made to show that resemblance in their form. Indeed the very word *type* means this, — having the *form* of the antitype. So Paul calls the tabernacle and all the Mosaic rites 'patterns' and 'figures' of heavenly things. (Heb. 9; 23, 24.) Had John said, 'I *plunge you into* water, but he that cometh after me will *pour upon you* the Holy Ghost,' where were the point and power of the antithesis? But if he said 'I indeed *pour upon* you clean water, but he shall *pour upon* you the Holy Ghost,' would not the symbol and the language lend to each other mutual and greatly augmented impressiveness and force? It seems to me in the very worst taste, — not impiety, as Mary would almost esteem it — for I do not believe our good brethren, the Baptists, mean any such thing, — but certainly bad taste to thrust in another figure so entirely incongruous, to destroy the whole grace and effect of this beautiful parallelism."

The whole party remained silent for a few moments, as if much impressed with the eloquence and force of the pastor's remarks. At length Mary spoke: —

"You have certainly put all this matter of John's baptism in a new light to me. I don't know what can be said in reply to it. Come, cousin Joseph, what do you think? Does 'silence give consent'? You let father do the talking and have almost nothing to say. Why is it — do tell us? Is it because you *have* nothing to say?"

"The truth is," replied Joseph, "that I have been so much surprised, not to say interested in some of the positions he has advanced, that I hardly felt like replying at all. I certainly shall not yet assent to them. Indeed, I may as well own that I am not quite satisfied with this mode of discussing the subject. We ought to have begun with ascertaining the meaning of the word *baptizo*, and having settled its meaning in classic usage, we should have had a sure key to its import in the New Testament. But in this way of reasoning the very postulates, or first principles of the argument, are denied us."

"That is," said Mr. Stanley, " you would insist on going to Homer and Aristotle to explain Jesus Christ; you would make heathenism, and not the law, our schoolmaster to bring us to him. I cannot think this will be recognized by plain people as a common sense way of proceeding. However, in its proper place, I will not refuse to accompany you to that school. We certainly are not afraid to inquire there for any light they have. Meanwhile, in closing this view of John's baptism at Jordan, there is one remark of some importance I wish to make, in the way of an inference from what has been said. It is to call your attention to the impropriety of the phrase our Baptist brethren so constantly use about '*following Christ* into the water,' or 'into the liquid grave.' "

" Why, Mr. Stanley, do you not think we may follow the example of our Lord in his baptism ? " inquired Nellie.

" Perhaps we may in the *fact* of his baptism, but it will not be the same baptism, nor received for the same reason."

" You mean, I suppose, that his was not *Christian* baptism ? " said Joseph.

" I do," was the reply.

" What ! " said Mrs. Mason, " not *Christian* baptism, when it was administered to Christ himself ? "

"No, ma'am; not any more than his circumcision and keeping the passover were Christian rites. For, in the first place, Christian baptism as an ordinance of the gospel which we are to observe was not then instituted, nor was it done till after our Lord's crucifixion, three and a half years later. (Matt. 28: 19; Mark 16: 16). Secondly, it had not the same meaning. It denoted simply repentance and a belief that the Messiah was about to come. (Acts 19: 4.) It implied no faith in anything peculiarly and distinctively Christian, such as the doctrine of the Trinity, the incarnation of Christ, his teaching and miracles, his atoning death, his resurrection and ascension, and the dispensation of the Spirit. It was simply a preparatory rite,—something leading to the door of the 'kingdom of heaven,' but not within that kingdom. Hence it was that Paul rebaptized the twelve disciples of John, whom he met at Ephesus. (Acts 19: 1–7). He found that they had never heard that there was such a thing as the Holy Ghost, showing that John did not baptize in the name of the Trinity. Now these were evidently good men, but they were not properly Christians. After Paul had explained the matter to them, they saw the defectiveness of the baptism they had received, though it was the very same that Christ himself had received, and were then rebaptized in the name of Jesus. So that if you were to follow Christ's example literally, and be baptized with his baptism, you would still be as far short of Christianity as these Ephesian disciples were, and need, as they did, to be baptized over again with a Christian baptism."

"What do you think then, sir, was the reason that Christ was baptized at all?" inquired Nellie. "He did not need the baptism of repentance, did he?"

"Certainly not, and for this reason John at first declined to administer it. But he was a Jew, as yet in a private and unofficial capacity, and of course when his nation was summoned by the prophet to the reception of that rite preparatory to the coming of the new kingdom of heaven, he felt it his duty to obey, as any other man would. 'It becometh us,' said he, 'to fulfill all righteousness;' that is, everything required of the nation. In the same way, he was circumcised, and kept the passover, and paid his taxes. As a sinless being he needed neither of the former, and as Lord of the temple might rightfully have pleaded exemption from the latter. (Matt. 17: 25). But he must honor the message sent to his people by God's prophet, and render, as a man, a perfect man's obedience in all respects."

"I have heard it asserted," said Joseph, "that Christ in his baptism was consecrated to the priesthood, and therefore must be sprinkled as the Jewish priests were required to be. (Ex 29: 4, 21.) But certainly this was not the case. He was not a priest in any ordinary sense. He never claimed to be, nor was he regarded as such by his disciples, or by the people generally. He called himself and was called by them a prophet. (Luke 7: 14; 13: 33; John 7: 40.) Nay, he *could* not have been a priest, because he was not of the priestly tribe, Levi, but of the tribe of Judah, as Paul so elaborately argues in the seventh chapter of Hebrews. How idle is it then to say that the righteousness which Christ wished to fulfill in his baptism was the law requiring a priest to be consecrated by sprinkling!"

"I think you are right, so far," said Mr. Stanley, "and I never like to hear that argument used. In any true sense in which Christ was a priest, he was made such 'not after the law of a carnal commandment, but after the power of an endless life.' (Heb 7 : 16.) Still, in a higher sense, Christ *was* a priest, a 'great High Priest' after the order of Melchisedec, that is a kingly priest without predecessors or successors; and into this he was inducted *at* his baptism by John, but *by* the baptism of the Holy Ghost, which followed and crowned that act of obedience."

"But that, after all," said Arthur, "is about the same argument, only put in a different way. As the Jewish priests must be consecrated to their office by washing and sprinkling, so Christ was inducted into his office by the baptism of the Holy Ghost, which was a descent upon him, *i. e.* a pouring or sprinkling from above. It was not literally obeying the law for the consecration of priests, but it was the *fulfillment* of that of which the law was a type and a promise."

"Your remark is very just, my son," replied Mr. Stanley. "And now there is one thing more that I wish to say about John's baptism, and then we must close our conversation unless we would fatigue Aunt Emily, for I fear we have stayed too long already. It is about his baptizing at Ænon 'because there was much water there.'" John 3 : 23.

"But that cannot prove immersion," said Mary, "if the baptism in Jordan does not."

"True," said her father. "The matter is of little consequence, only because we so often hear it referred to by Baptists, as if alone sufficient to decide the whole question. 'Why,' they ask, 'should the existence of much water at Ænon be made a reason for his baptizing there unless he wanted it for immersion?'"

"I should say, evidently," remarked Mary, "because it would, like the Jordan, accommodate the people that resorted there. But where was Ænon, father?"

"That is not certainly known. The word signifies the 'Springs,' and may have been given to it for the same reason that we often speak of Saratoga as the 'Springs,' because there *were* several springs there, which in the East would make it of course an important locality. The original words translated 'much water' are literally 'many waters,' that is, streams or rills running from the fountains. Dr. Robinson found a Salim to the east of Nabulus, the ancient Sychar, at which are two copious springs, and near to this he supposes Ænon to have been. John seems to have removed thither from Bethabara (or Bethania) on the Jordan (John 1: 28) for the purpose of accommodating the people who lived in that part of the country."

"But Dr. Hague," said Joseph, "refers to Rev. 14: 2, where the same words, 'many waters' denote the 'deep-sounding sea.'" (Reply to Cooke and Towne.)

"What if they did?" said Mary. "He don't pretend there was any such 'deep-sounding sea' at Ænon, does he? The roaring of the waves of the ocean under a storm, may by a bold, poetic figure be well styled 'the voice of many waters'; but what has that to do with the simple historical statement that John went to the 'Springs' to perform his ministry because there were many flowing rills or brooks there? One thing is certain: he did not go to find a river, a lake, or a sea, for the plain reason that no such thing was there."

"The expression, 'many waters,'" added Mr. Stanley, "is the same that is found in 2 Chron. 32: 3, 4, where it is said that King Hezekiah stopped up the 'waters of the fountains' which were without Jerusalem, saying, 'Why should the kings of Assyria come and find *much water?*' *i. e.*, supplies for their invading army. In Ezek.

19: 10, it denotes the little rills that water gardens. In Jer. 51: 13, it apparently refers to the numerous sluices and canals used for irrigating the plain around Babylon. Surely, to make immersion out of this expression in the passage before us, is to build up a large edifice out of very small materials."

"And now our conclusion for the evening is this: that the apostles to whom the commission to baptize was first given, having some of them been baptized by John, and having all seen and been familiar with his baptism, would inevitably, in the absence of all explanation, understand that the rite was to be administered in the same way. If he did it by sprinkling, after the general pattern of the Mosaic purifications, as I think has been proved to all reasonable apprehension, then they would infer that the Lord meant they should do the same. And now when shall we meet again?"

"Will to-morrow evening be too soon, Aunt Emily?" said Mary.

"No. Suit your own convenience," replied that lady.

And the session closed with that understanding.

CHAPTER III.

DIVERS BAPTISMS.

PROMPT as the stroke of the clock was the appearance of our friends in Mrs. Mason's sitting-room the next evening.

No long time was spent in preliminaries. The party gathered about the table as before, and Mary inquired, —.

"Who will tell just where we were when we closed last evening?"

"I think," said Arthur, "we were considering what means the apostles, who first received the commission to baptize, had of understanding it. Father's first reply was that they had themselves been baptized by John the Baptist, which opened the question as to the mode in which that baptism was administered. From the arguments he advanced, I for one was satisfied that it was done by sprinkling, not immersion."

"But that was not their only means of knowledge," said Joseph. "I would like here to suggest another of a different sort, — which you may if you please consider as a second. I refer to the fact that they must have been familiar with the *baptism of proselytes* on their reception to Judaism; and this, as we are expressly assured by the Jewish Rabbins, was done by immersion."

"I am glad you refer to that subject," said Mr. Stanley. "If you have it fresh in your mind, please present the facts as you understand them."

"I have had but a short time to look into it to-day, but the results I have gathered are briefly these: The question whether the practice of baptizing proselytes prevailed in the time of John, is one on which scholars are not agreed. Eminent names are found on both sides. The affirmative view is summarily stated by Prof. Alexander, of Scotland, under the following particulars. 1. The positive and unanimous testimony of the Jewish Rabbins. 2. The fact that John's baptism was regarded as no new thing. 3. That the dispute between John's disciples and a Jew about purifying, implied that they understood both Jesus and John as baptizing proselytes to their respective sects. 4. That Peter, on the day of Pentecost, addressing, among others, the proselytes, (Acts 2: 10) exhorted them to repent and be baptized, implying that they were already acquainted with that rite. 5. That the Essenes were in the habit, according to Josephus, (War, 2: 8. 7) of applying ' waters of purification ' to a convert to their sect. 6. That the same writer alludes to John's baptism, not as if John introduced it, but only gave to it a new meaning." Kitto, Bib. Cyclop.

"But all these," observed Mary, "except the 1st and 5th points, are substantially met by what father showed as to John's baptism. He did not claim it as anything new in its nature or form, but as springing out of the ancient ceremonial ritual. The same might be true with the baptism administered on the day of pentecost, which was now by the new commission made a Christian baptism. And I do not see why it is not equally reasonable to suppose that the Essenes derived their practice from the same source."

"All this I may admit," replied Joseph, "but the first point will remain unshaken. The testimony of the Jewish Rabbins as to the existence of proselyte baptism at the time of John, is, as Prof. Alexander remarks, 'unanimous.' I may add, it is equally decisive as to the *mode* of that baptism. They affirm that the candidate must be plunged wholly under water; that 'to leave one hand-breadth of his body unsubmerged would have vitiated the whole rite.' (Smith's Dic. Vol. 2: p. 943.) This simple statement, therefore, as it seems to me should be decisive. The Jews had long been in the habit of both circumcising and baptizing proselytes received to their faith; of course, the apostles were familiar with the rite under that form, and would necessarily infer that their own commission was to be interpreted in the same way."

"All which, if true, would only prove that they had seen the rite administered in more than one form, which is equally fatal to the exclusive ground of our Baptist brethren," said Mr. Stanley. "I am inclined to the belief that proselyte baptism did prevail at that time, and was administered both to the converts *and their children*, as the Rabbins with equal positiveness affirm, because, as Dean Alford remarks, 'the baptism or lustration of a proselyte on admission would follow as a matter of course, by analogy from the constant legal practice of lustration after all uncleannesses.' Com. on Matt. 3: 6.

"Nor do I care to call in question the statement of the Rabbins that this was done by immersion, although their authority, as we shall presently see, is not of the best. There was a special reason why it should be, which would not exist in other cases. Will Miss Nellie please turn to Num. 31: 21, and read the law as there recorded?"

She did so. "'And Eleazar the priest said unto the men of war, which went to the battle, This is the ordinance of the law which the Lord commanded Moses. Only the gold, and the silver, the brass, the iron, the tin, and the lead, everything that may abide the fire, ye shall make it go through the fire and it shall be clean; nevertheless it shall be purified with the water of separation: and all that abideth not the fire ye shall *make to go through the water.*'"

"This," continued Mr. Stanley, "was a statute applicable to objects obtained in war as a spoil from the enemy. It is the only instance of a distinctly required *immersion* to be found in the law, and evidently implies that what was thus obtained from foreign sources was pre-eminently unclean, and needed an extraordinary purification. Now, by a not very harsh figure, a proselyte received from the Gentiles might be conceived of as spoil won from an enemy, and subjected to this special and extraordinary mode of cleansing. And this very provision of the law is evidence to my mind that *such* a baptism would not be practiced in other cases; that the Jews themselves, the very seed of Abraham, would not have submitted to a rite whether administered by John or the apostles which would class them with the heathen."

"That is self evident," remarked Arthur, "and settles forever the objection so triumphantly urged by Baptists to the statement that the law never required *a Jew* to be immersed." Hague's Reply to Cooke and Towne.

"There is another consideration," resumed Mr. Stanley. "The Rabbins describe with great particularity the mode of baptizing converts practiced *in their day*. But that was several centuries after the time of John. The Mishna was completed about A. D. 220 and the two Talmuds from two to three centuries later. These affirm among other things that a proselyte was baptized *naked*. 'When the wound (from circumcision) was healed, he was stripped of all his clothes in the presence of the three witnesses who had acted as his teachers and who now acted as his sponsors, the "fathers" of the proselyte, and led into the tank or pool. As he stood there up to his neck in water, they repeated the great commandments of the law. These he promised and vowed to keep, and then, with an accompanying benediction he plunged under the water,' — that is, apparently, immersed himself. (Smith's Dict. vol. 2: p. 943.)

"Are we then to take this elaborate and cumbrous ceremonial — and I have cited to you but a small part of it — which may have been in use three centuries after Christ, as prevailing in all its fullness in the days of our Lord, and infer that the apostles made it the pattern of the rite they were to administer? If so, why is there no allusion to it in the New Testament? Take any one of the instances of baptism recorded in the Acts, and where have you any thing like this, the three sponsors, the stripping naked, the standing up to the neck in water, the repeating of the commandments and the self plunging at the end?"

"But," said Joseph, "the testimony of the Rabbins as to the fact of immersion, affirms it not of their own day only, but of previous ages."

"Not any more of this than of the other ceremonies mentioned. Indeed it is this very claim of great antiquity for the practice which throws doubt over their whole testimony. They asserted that proselyte baptism was as old as the times of Jacob (Gen. 35; 2) and Moses (Ex. 19; 10), and even corrupted the Targum on Ex. 12; 44 so as to read 'when thou hast circumcised *and baptized* him.' I suppose indeed they did just as partisans of a sect have always done in all religions, 'carrying back to an earlier age,' as Professor Plumptre remarks, the rules and decisions of their own times to invest them with a higher degree of authority. Rabbi Maimonides, the great oracle of the Jews in matters of religion, and the author of an elaborate commentary on the Mishna, was a Spanish Jew of the twelfth century, and is probably as trustworthy an expositor of the practices of his people in the time of Christ, as a similarly eminent Roman Catholic doctor would be as to the rites and usages of the apostolic churches. Prof. Stuart says, 'There are so many narratives in the Talmud which are gross mistakes and ridiculous conceits, that one hardly feels himself safe in trusting to any of its statements respecting facts that happened long before the period when this book was written.' (Bib. Rep. vol. 3: p. 352.) And Prof. Plumptre, 'The precepts of the Talmud may indicate the practices and opinions of the Jews from the second to the fifth century. They are very untrustworthy as to any other time.' Smith's Bib. Dic.

"Reviewing then the whole subject, we arrive at the decided probability that proselytes in the time of Christ were baptized in a manner conformable to the usual methods of ceremonial purification, as we have seen to be true of the baptism of John. Or if there was a special exception in their case, it was in consequence of a special statute imposed because of their Gentile origin. But even this, let it be remembered, expressly required them also to be 'purified with the water of separation' which, we know, was in all cases to be applied by sprinkling." Numb. 19: 20.

"I think you have made this matter very plain, sir," said Nellie. "The whole subject is evidently obscure, but so far as it can afford us any light, it seems to favor the view you have taken."

"So I think," said Arthur, "and now what is

your next point, father? We are upon the question as to what means the apostles had for correctly understanding the commission given them."

"My next remark is that they were *familiar with the Scriptures*," replied Mr. Stanley.

"That is, with the Old Testament," said Mary. "But what light does that throw on Christian baptism?"

"A good deal, as we have already seen," replied her father. "The Scriptures, were the text book of all knowledge to a Jew. They contained, first, the *law* with its minute directions on the subject of ritual purification. The twelve that were with Jesus had heard it read in the synagogues every Sabbath-day. Paul, that Hebrew of the Hebrews, had studied it at the feet of Gamaliel. And if there were any two things which were identical in the mind of a Jew, as an idea and its outward sign, they were PURIFICATION and SPRINKLING. Fourteen times are the words used in the law alone in this connection. And as they had read, so had they seen done in the temple. On the great day of expiation they had themselves gone thither to confess their sins and to behold the blood of the victim sprinkled upon the altar in atonement for their sins. Let a people thus be trained, both by law and practice, for fifteen hundred years, in this association of ideas, and they must necessarily, without special instruction to the contrary, on receiving a command to go forth and disciple the nations, and apply to them the symbol of moral cleansing, understand that it was to be done in like manner by sprinkling.

"Further, the Scriptures distinctly employ the word sprinkling to denote the peculiar effects of the new dispensation. Ezekiel, when predicting the restoration of the nation to the divine favor, in the days of the Messiah, represents Jehovah as saying, 'Then will I *sprinkle* clean water upon you, and ye shall be clean; from all your filthiness and from all your idols I will cleanse you. A new heart also will I give you, and a new spirit will I put within you, and I will take away the stony heart out of your flesh, and I will give you a heart of flesh' (Ezek. 26: 25, 26.). And in that most memorable prediction in Isa. 52: 53, the cleansing efficacy of his death is thus described. 'As many were astonished at thee, (his visage was so marred more than any man, and his form more than the sons of men), so shall he *sprinkle* many nations,' etc.

I do not suppose there is here any distinct reference to the rite of Christian baptism, but only to the general idea that by his death, and especially by the dispensation of the Spirit, the nations should obtain a moral purification."

"But you must be aware," interposed Joseph, "that the Septuagint version in this place instead of 'sprinkle,' reads 'shall be astonished,' making a correlative with 'were astonished' in the first clause; the idea being that as they should wonder at seeing his humiliation, so they should still more wonder at beholding his glory. Evidently this makes a smoother sentence and better sense. Gesenius understands it as meaning 'to exult'; *i. e.* he shall cause many nations to leap for joy."

"I am aware of this criticism," said Mr. Stanley, "but the weight of authority is against it. The word occurs some twenty times in the Old Testament, and in every other place it is translated sprinkle. Besides, it is a canon of criticism that as between two readings, one easy and the other difficult, the latter, other things being equal, is to be preferred, since it is more likely that if any change had been improperly made in the text, it would be from the latter to the former, than vice versa."

"Again, the apostles, if they read in the Septuagint version of the Scriptures, as from their quotations in the Gospels and Epistles is evident, must have found the word *baptizo* used there in connections which, as interpreted by their own law, would throw light on its meaning."

"But why not ascertain first its *classic* meaning," interposed Joseph, "the only true guide to its real signification?"

"Because," said Mr. Stanley, smiling at the persistency with which his nephew clung to that favorite artifice of the Baptists, "it is not the *classic* but the *Scripture* meaning we are after now. Probably the apostles knew nothing about the classics, but they had some clew to the meaning of their own Scriptures.

"The first instance of its use is in 2 Kings 5: 14, which relates the cleansing of Naaman the Syrian, at the Jordan. The question here is, not how should we with our Gentile eyes read this narrative, but how would a Jew read it? Here was a leper who was about to be cleansed of his leprosy. The prophet had commanded him, 'Go, wash'—*lousai*—a general word like our English one, specifying no particular mode—'seven times in Jordan.' Now no idea was more familiar to the Jewish mind than that of the cleansing of a leper. He was to be sprinkled seven times with the blood of a bird, to shave off all his hair, and to wash his clothes and his person with water. (Lev. 14: 7, 8). So the Jew reads, 'And Naaman went down'—*katebē*—a word never signifying to go under water—' and *baptized himself* in or at the Jordan seven times, according to the word of Elisha.' The sprinkling of the blood is omitted, perhaps because Naaman was a Gentile, possibly because there was no priest present to do it. Now what idea would this Jew reader derive from this as to the precise thing that Naaman did, and what therefore was the meaning of the word to baptize?"

"But," said Joseph, "we are told that the Hebrew word in this place is *yitbol*, from *tabal*, a word which does signify specifically to immerse."

"I grant it," said Mr. Stanley; "but that was not what the law required, nor the prophet had commanded, for even in the Hebrew the direction was not to immerse (*tabal*) but to wash (*rachatz*.) The LXX. seem to have chosen the word *ebaptisato* with reference to the intent of the requirement rather than to be an exact *verbal* equivalent to the original. They meant to say simply that Naaman did as he was bidden. Or we may interpret it with the learned Dr. Horner, thus: 'Accordingly he goes and dips into Jordan, and thereby obtains water which he dashes, sprinkles, or pours upon the spot seven times, with the intent and purpose of being thereby cleansed. Now, since for this time *tabal* includes the whole of this complex idea, it is rendered for the first and only time in the Old Testament by *baptizo*, since the action and effect was a literal baptism.' (Meth. Quar. Rev.)

"The next instances that I will cite occur in Dan. 4: 33, and 5: 21, where it is said that Nebuchadnezzar 'did eat grass as oxen, and his body was *wet — ebaphē —* with the dew of heaven.' It is true that the Greek word here used is from *bapto*, and not *baptizo*, the latter of which alone is applied to the Christian ordinance. But as the former is the root-verb from which the latter is derived, we may appropriately consult it as to the meaning of the derivative. The very statement of the fact shows here the import of the word. To be wet with the dews of heaven was to be suffused with drops of water. The claim of an immersion in this instance is a simple absurdity."

"So I should think," exclaimed Mary. "Pray cousin Joseph, what do you say to it?"

"I must candidly acknowledge," he replied, "that to make an immersion of this case is very difficult, but it is not impossible. Of course, it can be only figuratively such. Some think that the writer referred to the copiousness of the dews in that country, meaning to say that the monarch was as wet *as if* he had been dipped in dew. Dr. Carson, perhaps our most learned philologist, regards it as a rhetorical figure 'used to enliven the style.' (p. 38.) 'Do we not,' says he, 'every day hear similar phraseology? The man who has been exposed to a summer-plump,' *i. e.* I suppose, a sudden shower, 'will say that he has got a complete *dipping*. This is the very expression of Daniel. One mode of wetting is figured as another mode of wetting, by the liveliness of the imagination.'"

"All of which," said Mr. Stanley, "is evidently a strained effort to sustain his own theory that this Greek word never means anything but immersion. It finds no warrant whatever in the narrative, which is a simple, unpoetic statement of the fact that the king, as a judgment from heaven for his pride, was driven by his insanity into the field and adopted the life of a beast, without shelter from the night-dews, till his hair and nails had grown long. It was not the *quantity* of the wetting which was the important circumstance, but the *fact* that he was an outcast from his palace.

"The next occurrence of *baptizo* in the Septuagint is in Isa. 21 : 4; where, instead of 'fearfulness affrighted me,' as it is in the English version, the Greek has 'iniquity *baptizes* me.' The figure is that of a heavy burden or deluge of waters falling upon and overwhelming the soul. Nothing but absolute violence can make out an immersion here.

"The book of Judith presents the next instance."

"But that was no part of the Bible, father, was it?" asked Arthur.

"The Jews did not admit it and the other books known as the Apocrypha into their canon, because they had no Hebrew original, or because they were not regarded as inspired. They were however in the Septuagint, as they are in the Latin Vulgate, and would of course be familiar to those who read the Septuagint. That fact is sufficient for our present purpose, which is to ascertain the meaning of the word *baptizo*, as the apostles had become accustomed to it in that venerable version.

"In Judith 12: 7; it is said that that lady 'went out nightly to the valley of Bethulia, and baptized herself — *ebaptizeto* — in the camp at a fountain of water.' Bethulia, a fortified village in the north of Palestine, was besieged by an Assyrian army. Judith, a beautiful and pious widow, undertook its deliverance. Accompanied by her maid she goes to the enemy's camp and asks to be conducted to their general Holofernes. She offers to show him the approaches to the village, asking only that till he is ready to march she may go out into the valley to perform her ablutions, and to pray in the night. He grants her request, and she accordingly remains there three days, going each night to the valley, and washing herself at the fountain. These circumstances show the unreasonableness of supposing that this washing was immersion. A refined, chaste woman, would not, if allowed, have thus exposed herself in a military camp; she would not have washed *in* a fountain from which the soldiers obtained their supplies for drinking and cooking; and the preposition *epi*, translated 'at' never means *in*."

"And yet," said Mary, "I suppose Dr. Carson insists that she did. Do tell us, Joseph, how he makes it out."

"I do not recollect precisely," said the latter, "and I have not his book at hand."

"I can tell you," replied her father. "The passage evidently troubles him. First he says she immersed herself *in* the fountain. Afterwards he asks, 'Was it utterly impossible to have a conveniency for bathing near a fountain? On the contrary was it not very probable that stone troughs or other vessels were usually provided at fountains for bathing and washing clothes?' Again, 'Even were it certain that at this fountain there was no such provision, might not some person have supplied her with a vessel? (p. 78.) 'Was it not usual to have stone troughs at fountains for the purpose of watering cattle?' (p. 456.) But notwithstanding all these suppositions, he finally comes back to the first position, that she actually immersed herself *in* the fountain. The fact that bands of soldiers were stationed to guard the fountain (ch. 7: 7), does not stand in the way; he sees nothing in this to make it indelicate for her thus to expose herself."

"Oh brother," interrupted Mrs. Mason, "you surely are not in earnest now! No sensible man, — not to say no Christian minister, could insist on such an unworthy position."

"Indeed, I am in sober earnest, as much so as any one can be in relating the extravagant assertions of a man crazed by one idea. Nay, I have not told you all. 'I care not in the least degree,' says he, 'how any one may decide as to views of delicacy in this matter. However indelicate any one may choose to consider the conduct of Judith, the fact is in proof, and I will not suffer views of delicacy to question it.'" p. 318.

"And does he give no other proof than simply the alleged meaning of the word *baptizo?*" asked Miss Ashton.

"No; that is the whole. And yet this is nothing to what he says he can prove by the word. 'I care not,' he says, 'if there had not been a fountain in all Bethulia; she might have been immersed without it. If from other places, I prove that *immerse* is the meaning of the word, this in every situation will provide the water.' (p. 319.) 'Had Judith been most rigorously treated, and confined to her tent, when she is said to be baptized for purification, I will make the word find her water.' (p. 457). 'Our reason for believing that Judith was *immersed* is, that the historian tells us that she was *immersed*,' *i. e.* baptized."

"But does this man imagine that persons in their senses will accept these specimens of reasoning?" exclaimed Mary.

"Apparently. And he seems quite indignant that they do not. 'My opponents are more unreasonable with me,' says he, 'than the Israelites were with Moses: *they* murmured when they had no water!' (p. 459.) And in one case, when declaiming against the arguments of the venerable and scholarly Dr. Miller of Princeton, this Dr. Carson cries out, 'Were the angel Gabriel to hesitate, I would order him to school!'" p. 384.

"I confess," said Joseph, "that such dogmatism and profanity are shocking. No candid mind can fail of being disgusted by them. Still, it would be an error on the other side to be repelled by them from the really sound arguments which he advances. Dr. Carson is a very able man, and is regarded as a tower of strength by our churches and ministers."

"I am aware of it," said Mr. Stanley, "hence my reference to his work. It is published by the

'American Baptist Publication Society,' which of course is the highest imprimatur of the denomination.

"The only remaining instance in which the word occurs in the Septuagint is in Ecclesiasticus 31: 35: 'He that is baptized — *baptizomenos* — from a dead body and again touches it, what profit has he from his washing?'. What this baptism was, we learn from Numb. 19: 14–22. It was to be *sprinkled* with the water of separation, to wash his clothes, and to wash himself — *rachatz* — in water. Nothing in the words themselves, and nothing in the law requires the sense of immersion, or creates the least probability that such was the mode employed. To say that the bathing here mentioned was an immersion is simply to beg the whole question.

"Such then," continued Mr. Stanley, "was the teaching of the ancient Scriptures, both as to the idea involved in a ritual purification, and the term 'baptism,' chosen to express it. Such was the help afforded the apostles for the right understanding of our Lord's command to go and baptize all nations. Never in the law had they seen an immersion commanded; never in the use of the word had they seen an immersion related.

All their instructions from this source had been to the opposite effect. They had seen sprinklings in the Mosaic ritual, and sprinkling as the figurative representation of the work of the Messiah. They had read of the leprous Naaman baptizing himself seven times at the river, of Nebuchadnezzar baptized with the dews, of the prophet baptized with an overwhelming sense of iniquity, of the pious Hebrew widow baptizing herself before prayer at a drinking fountain in the military camp, and of a person who had touched a dead body baptized with the sprinkled water of purification. What then must have been their idea of the meaning of the word? What of the work they were to do in fulfilling their great commission?"

"I do not see how any one can resist the force of this reasoning," remarked Arthur. "The Bible has always been one of the greatest educators of men. Our English version, which we have had in its present form less than three hundred years, just about the same space of time that the Jews before Christ had had the Septuagint, is conceded by all scholars to have done more to fix the meaning and use of the words employed in it than any other one thing. How potent then must this book have been in determining the import of words among a people to whom it was the source of all authority, secular as well as sacred,— not only their Bible, but also the Constitution and Statute Book of the state!"

"And this brings us to a fourth remark under this first general head," said Mr. Stanley; "and that is that the apostles and their associates had themselves *been accustomed to use the word baptizo and its derivatives*. The commission was a new one, but the words employed in it were already familiar. Let us see to what things they had been wont to apply them.

"On a certain occasion our Lord was invited to dine with a Pharisee, and Luke (ch. 11: 38,) says that his host 'marveled that he had not first *baptized himself — ebaptisthē —* before dinner.' What was this act which had been omitted, and which was called by the Evangelist a *baptism?*"

"Dr. Carson and all Baptists say it was an immersion," answered Joseph.

"Yes, and they prove it only from the word itself, the meaning of which is the very thing in dispute. Mark also makes the following statement (ch. 7: 4.). 'And when they' *i. e.* all the Jews, 'come from the market except they *baptize themselves — baptizontai —* they eat not.' Now in opposition to the claim that this was a custom of immersion I allege, first, that it is a pure *assumption*. There is not a particle of evidence in support of a practice so burdensome, so wasteful of time, and so detrimental to health, which must have amounted to taking a plunge bath never less than three times a day, and in case of men called from home by business or pleasure, several times more. Secondly, it is highly *improbable*. Where, for instance, could such an habitual dipping have been performed? In such a country as Palestine, where most of the streams are dry for months together, access could not generally be had to brooks or rivers. Cisterns and wells were not places to bathe in. Baths large enough for such a purpose could not have been usual, nor could water in sufficient quantities have been had if they were. At public feasts, or where a large number of guests were assembled, as may have been the case in this instance when Jesus dined with the Pharisee, how unreasonable to suppose that they all went and stripped themselves and took a plunge bath preparatory to coming to the table. On the other hand, what we do know of the domestic arrangements of the

Jews, points to a very different method of ablution. Take the house of the bridegroom in Cana, who was evidently one of the wealthier class, and what do we find as to its provision for performing this and the other ceremonial washings of the Jews? Why, 'six water pots of stone containing two or three firkins'—from 15 to 20 gals.—apiece. Certainly no person ever plunged himself bodily into one of these. When their contents were to be used, they were 'drawn out' (verse 8). And, generally, the custom of bathing in the East, unless it were in a pool or river, (and not always with that exception), was performed by standing beside a bath and having the water *poured upon* the bather by an attendant. 'On ancient vases,' says Dr. Wm. Smith, (Dic. of Gr. and Rom. Ant. p. 184,) 'on which persons are represented bathing, we never find anything corresponding to a modern bath, in which persons can stand or sit, but there is always a round or oval basin resting on a stand, by the side of which those who are bathing are represented standing undressed and washing themselves, as is seen in the accompanying wood-cut taken from Sir William Hamilton's vases.'

WATER POT.

A GREEK BATH.

"Is it not very singular if these numerous and habitual washings were always, by 'all the Jews,' performed by immersion, that we never in all the Bible find any mention of a vessel in which it was done? Their dwellings and furniture are frequently described with more or less particularity, their beds and tables and culinary utensils, their mills for grinding, their ovens and kneading troughs, their bottles and pitchers and lamps, but never any where the article which, on this assumption, must have been in more constant use than any other, the *bath-tub*? In a careful description of a modern Baptist church, is the baptistery the one thing which is invariably left out?"

"In order to show that the Jews may have immersed themselves," said Joseph, "we may refer to a like custom among the Abyssinians. Mr. Bruce informs us that the sect called the *Kemmont*, 'wash themselves from head to foot, after coming from market or any public place where they may have touched any one of a sect different from their own, esteeming all such unclean.' (Rob. Cal. page 142). And Dr. Carson asks, 'Is it strange to find the superstitious Pharisees immersing themselves or their couches for purification?'"

"To this I have two replies to make," said Mr. Stanley. "One is that the customs of the Jews cannot be inferred from an Abyssinian sect. The other is that Bruce does not say the Kemmont immersed themselves. They 'washed themselves from head to foot.' Washing even the whole body is one thing, immersion quite another."

"Dr. Gale," said Joseph, "understands the passage in Mark as meaning that the Jews dipped the *articles* they had bought in the market, not themselves; and cites several ancient versions of the New Testament, the Syriac, Arabic, etc., in support of this view."

"But there is no more evidence of this practice among them than of personal immersions," replied the pastor; "besides this is to put an impossible meaning on the Greek text."

"Do you not think, sir, that it may mean that the Pharisees simply washed their *hands* after coming from the market, and before eating, and that this was done, as is most natural, by dipping them in water?" asked Miss Ashton.

"Undoubtedly the practice was that of washing the hands," replied Mr. Stanley, "as the verses immediately preceding show. 'When they saw some of his disciples eat bread with defiled, that is to say, with unwashen hands, they found fault. For the Pharisees and all the Jews except they wash their hands oft, eat not.' But washing the hands, even if it was immersion, was not an immersion of the whole body. If this is all that the Baptists contend for, the controversy is ended. A little hand-font holding a gallon would avail for this as well as a baptistery containing hogsheads.

"It is an important fact, that among different nations, and in different ages, entire purity has been represented by applying water to only a part of the body. Thus the Hebrews, Greeks and Romans, were accustomed to wash the hands in token of innocence. Among the Jews when the body of a murdered man was found, and the murderer could not be discovered, the elders of the city were required to wash their hands over a slain heifer in token of their innocence of the murder. If entire purity may not be represented by a *partial* washing, the elders should have immersed themselves. David says, 'I will wash my hands in innocency,' and Pilate took water, and washed his *hands*, saying, 'I am innocent of the blood of this just person.'

"But immersion, whatever may be customary with us, was not the usual way of washing the hands in the East. That method was undoubtedly the same that was in existence a thousand years before, in the days of 'Elisha the son of Shaphat, which *poured water upon the hands* of Elijah' (2 Kings 3:11), and which with all the tenacity of eastern customs continues to this day. Thus Dr. Thomson, in describing an oriental meal says, 'Of course after such a meal'— (in this respect only the custom seems to have changed; it was formerly before eating) 'washing the hands and mouth is indispensable — and the *ibrick* and *tusht*, their pitcher and ewer, are al-

Oriental Washing of Hands.

Page 87.

ways brought, and the servant with a napkin over his shoulder *pours on your hands*. If there is no servant they perform this office for each other. Great men have those about them whose special business it is to pour water on their hands.'" See the cut on the opposite page.

"Nothing can be more satisfactory than this," said Mary. "And will you now, in this connection, explain what we are to understand by the other things mentioned, in the same verse, viz: 'the washing of pots and cups and brazen vessels and tables'?"

"These washings," replied her father, "called *baptisms* in the original, were a part of the ceremonial purifications so common among the Jews. As to all but the last, the only hint we have as to the manner in which they were done, is afforded us by the severe rebuke administered by Christ, for the hypocrisy of the Pharisees in making clean the outside of the cup and the platter, while within they were full of impurity. (Matt. 23: 25.) It would seem from this that whatever was the mode employed, it was applied *only to the outside*, else the language of our Saviour would not hold, and if so, that it was not immersion, which would, of course, cleanse the inside and outside alike. As to the articles last mentioned, called in our translation 'tables'—*klinai*—what do you suppose they were?"

"Why, brother," said Mrs. Mason, "what could they have been but the pieces of furniture used at meals for supporting the food and dishes, as with us?"

"No," said Mr. Stanley, "they were something far different from ours. In fact they were not *tables* at all, but rather beds or divans upon which persons reclined while *at* the table. The cut opposite, copied from Calmet's Dictionary, will give you a better idea of them than any verbal description.

"'The Hebrews,' says he, 'anciently sat at table, but afterwards imitated the Persians and Chaldeans who reclined on table-beds or divans while eating. The reader is requested to notice the construction of the tables, viz. three tables so set together as to form one. Around these tables are placed, not seats, but couches or beds, one to each table; each of these beds being called *clinium*, three of these united to surround the three tables formed the *triclinium* (three beds). These beds were formed of mattresses stuffed, and were often highly ornamented. Observe the

The Triclinium, or Ancient Table-Couches.

attitude of the guests, each reclining on his left elbow, and therefore using principally his right hand, that only or at least chiefly being free for use. Observe also that the feet of the person reclining being towards the external edge of the bed, they were much more readily reached by any body passing, than any other part of the person so reclining!'

"This attitude at meals is certified not only by historical testimony, but by the express language of the Scriptures, and by the circumstances recorded on several occasions. The phrase 'to sit at meat,' and kindred terms are, in the original, to *recline*, as on a couch. (Matt. 26: 7, 20; Mark 14: 18; 16: 4; Luke 7: 36; 14: 8; 24: 30; John 13: 23.) It was while thus reclining that the 'woman that was a sinner,' and afterwards Mary, the sister of Lazarus, came behind our Lord and washed and anointed his feet. (Luke 7: 38; John 12: 3). So also when he washed the feet of his disciples. John 13: 5.

"Now I ask you to look at this bulky apparatus for meals, and persuade yourselves, if you can, that the Pharisees were in the habit of actually immersing it totally in water for the purposes of ceremonial purification. I do not say it was impossible; the couches *may* have all been taken apart and immersed piece by piece; the mattresses and cushions, often richly embroidered, *may* have been dipped one by one, and all this frequently and habitually, but who in his senses can possibly believe it? No law required it; there was rarely, if ever, a bath or other place where it could have been done; and there is no evidence that in fact it ever was done. To affirm it is to show to what urgent straits they are driven who maintain that the word baptism always and only means immersion, and upon what amazing grounds they build the walls which exclude from membership in Christ's church and communion at his table all who are unimmersed."

"How do Baptists usually explain this matter?" inquired Nellie.

"Generally, I think," said Joseph, "by maintaining that the couches here intended were not those on which persons reclined at meals, but the ordinary beds on which they slept, and which were often only a mat laid upon the floor. These could be taken up and carried (Matt. 9: 6; John 5: 5—12), and of course could be easily immersed."

"But the word is not restricted to this class

of couches," rejoined Mr. Stanley. "It does not say, the washings of pots and cups and beds small enough to be taken up and carried. Besides, the connection in which it stands shows it was meant to refer to these table-couches. The mention of these things grew out of what took place at a meal, and occurs in a description of the practices of the Jews relating to meals. Nobody, if not striving to maintain a point, would ever think of any other reference in this connection. Accordingly, many Baptists, to escape from a position in which all authorities are against them, resort to a variety of other suppositions, all of which are marvels of conjecture. Dr. Carson himself, though contending for the little portable mats, guesses many other things. 'Whatever might have been their size, they might easily be immersed *in a pond.*' p. 400. 'The couches might have been made to be *taken to pieces*, in order to their more convenient immersion, and were this necessary it is a valid solution.'" p. 451.

"I once heard," remarked Arthur, "a Baptist Doctor of Divinity say that the dining rooms of the Jews might have been made water-tight and the water have been admitted by pipes, or brought in by hand and poured upon the couches, till they were wholly immersed in it."

"And what did you reply, my son, to that suggestion?"

"I said I would not reply to it at all. I would let the difficulty and the explanation go together, and leave it to men's common sense to judge of them."

"A very appropriate answer, I think. Indeed, it astonishes me beyond measure to see to what methods of reasoning our brethren will resort to uphold their theory. 'The opponents of immersion, says Carson, are constantly calling on us to prove that there were in such and such places things necessary for dipping. Mr. E.' (one of his opponents) 'gauges the reservoirs and wells of Jerusalem to show their insufficiency for immersion. He may then call on me to find a place sufficient to immerse a couch. But I will go on no such errand. If I have proved the meaning of a word, I will believe the Spirit of God who tells me that the Pharisees baptized their beds, and leave the superstition and industry of the devotees to find or make such a place.—If I could prove that there was at Jerusalem a pond that could immerse the high church of Glasgow, I would certainly bring forward my proof, but I would as certainly disclaim the necessity." pp. 73, 74.

"And why not necessary, father," said Mary.

"Oh, because the *word, baptize,* settles it! 'Though it were proved' says he, 'that the couches COULD NOT BE IMMERSED, I would not yield an inch of the ground I have occupied!'

"But let us proceed with our illustrations of the use which Christ himself and the apostles had been wont to make of the words in question. On two occasions he applied them to his own approaching sufferings and death. 'I have a baptism to be baptized with, and how am I straitened till it be accomplished!' (Luke 12: 50.) So to the two ambitious disciples who wanted places of honor in his kingdom, he said, 'Are ye able to drink of the cup that I shall drink of and to be baptized with the baptism that I am baptized with?' (Matt. 20: 22, 23.) I do not suppose that they understood him then, in these sayings; indeed, when he spoke of his death in the most explicit manner, they knew not what to make of it. But the time came when they knew what he meant. It was 'on that dark and doleful night' when they went down with him into Gethsemane, and saw the heavy cloud of anguish and horror settling upon him; when they heard him cry that if it were possible the cup might pass from him, and saw his sweat, like great drops of blood, falling down to the ground. It was when they beheld his sacred countenance stained with the trickling streams drawn forth by his thorny crown, and saw the mingled blood and water which, at the thrust of the Roman spear, poured from his wounded side. Then it was that they learned what was that *baptism* of sufferings and death, which he was to endure, and which, they too, according to his promise should afterwards share, the 'martyr baptism,' as the primitive Christians used to call it, in which they were crucified with Christ."

"But what objection is there," asked Joseph, "to our conceiving of these sufferings as something into which he was immersed? We often use a similar phrase, ' to be plunged into grief, to be immersed in woes, etc.' Of course, in whatever way we view it, the baptism was a figurative one, and why is not this the most natural way of accounting for the figure?"

"Possibly we might so conceive of it, if there was any shadow of warrant for it. But never, in all the Scriptures, I venture to say, is there any thing like this in reference to the sufferings of our Lord. On the contrary, they are always represented as something that were to *come upon him*. ' He was stricken, smitten of God, and afflicted. He hath borne our griefs and carried our sorrows, the chastisement of our sins was upon him, — the Lord hath laid *upon him* the iniquity of us all.' The divine displeasure, which, as our substitute, he bore, is represented as something 'poured out,' and even in his own last conscious pang, he is said to have '*poured out* his soul unto death.' (Isa. 53: 12.) I do not mean, of course, that these expressions have any reference to the form of baptism, but only that they go to shape our thoughts as to what was in our Lord's mind when he took that word as descriptive of his atoning sorrows. To conceive of him as plunging into a pool of woe and death, is not only wholly unwarranted, but, to my mind, repellant to every sacred instinct and feeling.[1]

---

[1] Dr. J. W. Dale, author of the recent able and valuable works on "Classic," "Judaic," and "Johannic Baptisms," derives this figure from a very frequent use of *baptizo* in classic Greek, to denote the effect of *drinking from a cup*, that effect depending upon the nature of the draught. It may be drunkenness, or sleep, or stupor, or death. "A comparison," says he, "of the passages of Scripture relating to this subject with one another, confirms the relation suggested. In John

"I remark lastly, under this head, the apostles had heard of the *baptism of the Holy Ghost*, nay, had been promised that they should themselves very speedily receive it. (Luke 24: 49; John 20: 22; Acts 1: 8.) This was one of the topics of John's preaching, as it had been of all the prophets before him. Whether any of the twelve witnessed the descent of the Spirit upon Christ at his baptism is doubtful, but with the account of it they must have been familiar. Before they went forth to execute their commission, that wonderful promise to themselves was fulfilled on the day of pentecost. So that they must have had the best of all instruction as to the meaning of the thing called baptism, the direct illumination and experience of the Spirit himself.

"Now the *form* of this baptism they knew was not that of immersion. By 'form,' here, I refer, of course, not to the invisible work itself, for

---

18: 11, 'The *cup* which my Father hath given me, shall I not drink it?' the cause only is brought to view. In Luke 12: 50, 'I have a *baptism* to be baptized with,' the result is only brought to view. But in Mark 10: 38, 'Can ye drink of the *cup* that I drink of, and be baptized with the *baptism* that I am baptized with?' both the cause (drinking of the cup) and the effect of that drinking (baptism) are brought together. . . We therefore say that the cup which the Saviour drank was filled with atoning sufferings and that the baptism consequent upon drinking that cup was into expiatory death." "Cup and Cross" p. 24. Compare with this the Greek usage shown on p. 187.

that, being spiritual, has no form. I mean the mode divinely chosen to represent that work to men, whether by visible manifestations, or by verbal description. In no case, whatever, was it presented to man under the form of an immersion, as something into which one is plunged, but always as that which *comes down upon* him from above himself.

"These visible manifestations were two-fold. At the baptism of Jesus, Luke says, (ch. 3: 22,) 'the Holy Ghost descended in a bodily shape like a dove upon him.' Doubtless it was a luminous appearance assuming the form of this bird, and gliding downward with a gentle hovering motion upon the head of our Lord. On the day of pentecost, it was in the shape of 'cloven tongues like as of fire,' sitting on the head of each of the disciples. Acts 2: 3.

" The verbal expressions describing the baptism of the Spirit are various. Perhaps the most common of all is to *pour* and to *pour out*. 'I will pour out of my Spirit upon all flesh.' 'I will pour out in those days of my Spirit.' (Joel 2: 28, 29.) 'On the Gentiles was poured out the gift of the Holy Ghost (Acts 10: 45.) See also Isa. 32: 15; 44: 3; Ezek. 29: 39; Zech. 12:

7

10. In Acts 2 : 23, the expression is 'hath *shed forth.*' (Ezek. 11 : 5.) 'The Spirit of the Lord *fell upon* me.' So in Acts 11 : 15. Similar terms are used in describing the effects of the Spirit's operation. 'He shall *sprinkle* many nations.' (Isa. 52 : 15.) 'I will sprinkle clean water upon you.' (Ezek. 36 : 25.) 'Descend' and 'descending,' to 'be on' and to 'put upon,' to 'abide upon,' to 'rest upon' and to 'sit upon,' to 'anoint,' to 'seal,' etc., are other phrases of a similar character.

"Glance now through all these modes of representation, by visible symbols and by verbal expression, to set forth the baptism of the Holy Spirit, and where do you find any thing that in the remotest degree resembles an immersion? To thrust such an idea into the midst of this sacred symbolism seems to me, I confess, not only unwarranted but something shocking. And yet this is the way that our Baptist brethren have *dared*—I do not think the word too strong— to translate the awful words of John, making him say, 'He shall immerse you in the Holy Ghost and fire'! Nay, because the American Bible Society would not go with them in this innovation, to call it by no worse name, they must withdraw their co-operation from it, breaking the blessed fellowship of work in giving God's Word to the world, and set up an institution of their own in which they can manipulate the inspired language to conform to and uphold the unwarranted assumptions of their sect!"

"You speak, strongly, brother," said Mrs. Mason. "They were certainly good men who did that."

"I do not question it, nor do I speak unkindly, but the proceeding itself I regard as most reprehensible."

"But," said Joseph, "is not the preposition used in the verse you have referred to, *en*, and would it not therefore, if translated literally, read, 'He shall baptize you in the Holy Ghost?'"

"It is true," replied Mr. Stanley, "that the word *en* is used, but this preposition in Greek has a far wider signification than our English *in*. One of its commonest uses is to denote the agency or instrumentality *by* which an act is performed, especially when that agent or instrument is a *person*. So you will see by looking at any good Lexicon, Robinson's, for example. Instances innumerable might be cited, a few of which are these. "He casts out devils *by* the prince of the devils.' 'There is none other name *whereby* we must be saved.' 'He will judge the world in righteousness *by* that man whom he hath ordained.' 'This kind goeth not out but *by* prayer and fasting.' 'If thou shalt confess *with* thy mouth.' 'Overcome evil *with* good,' etc. No one would think of substituting *in* in these passages."

"After all, uncle, you must concede that the outpouring of the Spirit was not a *literal* baptism; it is only *figuratively called so*," said Joseph.

"Not literal! Pray what authority have you for saying this? It was not water baptism, I grant, but it was nevertheless *a* baptism, as really as if it had been. There was a literal act performed by the Spirit of God; that act was shown to men in a certain manner; and that literal act, so manifested, is called a *baptism*. Our Lord himself expressly applies to it that name, and will you question the propriety of his language?"

"But there certainly was an immersion there," persisted Joseph. "Are we not told that the Spirit came from heaven as a rushing, mighty wind, and filled all the place where the disciples were sitting? And if it filled the room they were immersed in the Spirit, were they not?"

"No; it says a *sound* like as of a rushing, mighty wind came, and it filled, etc. Not the Spirit, nor even a wind, but a sound *as of* a wind. If there was an immersion then, it was an immersion in *sound* and in nothing more substantial. So in the formation of their religious beliefs, men are often led by a *sound* of words to holding opinions as empty as itself."

A laugh went round the table at Joseph's expense; when Nellie, as if to cover his chagrin, asked:

"What do you think, Mr. Stanley, is meant by the baptism with fire which John predicted? Was it the same thing as the baptism of the Spirit, symbolized in the 'cloven tongues like as of fire,' which appeared on the heads of the apostles?"

"I think not," he replied, "though I am aware that many commentators so interpret it. If you will carefully examine the prophecy of Malachi, you will find that it contained the texts, so to speak, from which John preached. The Messiah was to come in a twofold character as a Purifier of his people, and a Punisher of his foes. The former he would 'purge as gold and silver, that they might offer to the Lord an offering in righteousness,' (ch. 3: 3). The latter, says the prophet, 'shall be stubble, and the day that cometh shall burn them up, that it shall leave them neither root nor branch'; (ch. 4: 1). The preaching of John but reiterated this. He shall baptize *you* — including under the same word both good and bad, as they came intermingled to hear him — 'with the Holy Ghost and with fire.' This was precisely what our Lord himself taught. 'He that believeth shall be saved, he that believeth not shall be damned.' We can scarcely think of looking for the figure of the baptism under this appalling language, or if we must, we may possibly find it under the prophet's conception of a fiery tempest from heaven, falling upon and consuming the dry remnants of the harvest field, gleaned of the wheat already gathered into the garner.

"We have now," said Mr. Stanley, "completed our answer to the question, 'What means had the apostles for understanding the commission given them?' They had seen the baptism of John and the baptism of proselytes; they had learned the nature and circumstances of the baptisms mentioned in their Scriptures; they had seen what sorts of acts were called by that name by our Lord himself and by their associates; and they had seen and received the baptism of the Holy Spirit. In all these classes of acts, and in every instance under them, they had seen and known it, so far as we can discover, only as a pouring or sprinkling, never as an immersion. This was their *education* in the use of the word 'baptism,' and their preparation for understanding what their Lord meant when he commanded them to go, teach, and baptize all nations.

"And now we must close our session for the evening."

CHAPTER IV.

PRACTICE AND TEACHING OF THE APOSTLES.

"WHAT shall we take up this evening?" said Mary Stanley, when our friends were next gathered around Mrs. Mason's table.

"Shall it be the classic usage of *baptizo?*" inquired Joseph, with a smile.

"Not quite yet, I think," replied his uncle. "We have hitherto been considering, mostly, what means the apostles had of understanding their commission. The next thing in order, I will suggest, is the inquiry, *How did they understand it?* And this we are to learn from two sources, first, what they *did*, and secondly what they *said*."

"Yes," answered Mrs. Mason, "that is a very reasonable view of the subject. If we find that, as a matter of fact, they did immerse persons in baptism, that is evidence that they so understood it."

"And if not, not," added Mr. S.

"Well, then," said Mary, "what did they do? What was the first baptism they administered?"

"It was that of the three thousand converts on the day of pentecost," said Joseph. "Will you read us the account, Nellie? It is in the second of Acts."

Miss Ashton read it.

"Now here are a number of things to look at," said Mr. Stanley. "And first, the *time*. When was that, Arthur?"

"'Pentecost' means the 'fiftieth day,' and was reckoned from the 16th of Nisan, which was the second day of the passover. This would bring it, ordinarily, about the 20th of May."

"Next the place, Mary?"

"That is not definitely stated. They were all 'in one place.' Was it the temple?"

"Probably not; more likely in the 'upper room' where they had been accustomed to meet since Christ's ascension. (ch. 1: 13.) The large gathering of the people *may* have been in the temple, but was more probably in the open space called the Xystus, constructed in the time of Antiochus Epiphanes, for athletic exercises and sports, after the manner of the Greeks. (2 Macc. 4: 9-12.) It seems to have been in the Tyropœan valley, west of the temple, extending perhaps a little way up the slope of Mt. Zion. Now for the baptism itself. How was it, Joseph?"

"By immersion, we say, of course."

"And what evidence have you of this?"

"I do not know that there is any except what the word itself affords. The record says they were baptized, and that is the same thing as to say they were immersed."

"But to this there are three insuperable objections; there was no place to do it in; no provision of baptismal garments; and no sufficient time."

"As to the place," said Joseph, "I see no difficulty. Jerusalem abounded in cisterns and fountains, besides its large pools, the reservoir under the temple, and the aqueduct of Solomon. Dr. Robinson, who studied the subject with great care, says, 'The Holy City would appear always to have had a full supply of water for its inhabitants in ancient and in modern times. In the numerous sieges, to which in all ages it has been exposed, we nowhere read of any want of water within the city.'"

"Yes, a full supply for drinking, but not for the immersion of three thousand persons in one afternoon. Take those places in detail. Cisterns were very abundant, but they were, says Robinson, 'from twenty to seventy-five feet deep, with, usually, only a round opening at the top, sometimes built up with stonework above, and furnished with a curb, and a wheel for the bucket, so that they had, externally, much the appearance of a well.' Not very good places for immersion, certainly. Take the pools. Those called Solomon's were eight miles distant from the city, between Bethlehem and Hebron, whose waters were conveyed in a covered aqueduct, a few inches only in diameter, to the reservoirs beneath the temple. The latter were huge caverns cut in the solid rock, containing supplies for the temple-service. There was no public access to them, and nobody would have been allowed, by bathing in them, to pollute the waters to be used in the sanctuary. The pools of Gihon, Upper and Lower, in the valley of Hinnom, and the pool of Hezekiah within the city, were vast stone reservoirs, from eighteen to forty feet deep, in which persons, possibly, might swim, but into which they could no more wade for immersion, than into the distributing reservoir of the Croton, in New York. Bethesda, or what goes by that name now, was then probably but a dry ditch or fosse constituting part of the fortifications of the temple. Siloam, which may have been the true Bethesda of our Lord's time, was too small to have made such an immersion in it practicable. The brook Kidron rarely had any water in it except in the winter, and then was a mad, muddy torrent rushing along a narrow gorge which sinks five hundred feet, perpendicularly, in the space of less than a mile. Jordan was eighteen miles distant. Now, I do not say there *could* not have been a place where these three thousand persons might be immersed in one afternoon, but certainly no such place is known, or has been found by the most diligent explorers of the antiquities of that city. Show us such a place, or give us some clew to it in the Bible, or Josephus, or somewhere else, before you ask us to believe that such a thing actually occurred, or deny us our place in the church of God because we do not believe it.

"Then, there is the same difficulty as to baptismal clothing we had in connection with John's baptism. Very many of these converts were strangers in Jerusalem, and cannot be supposed to have been provided with changes of garments. Either they remained in their wet clothes during the service, or were immersed naked, neither of which is supposable.

"Nor was there any sufficient time for such a task as this. It must have been well on in the afternoon before it commenced, and no computation I ever heard of could make it reasonable that twelve men should have gone through such a work during the remaining hours of the day. I know well what exploits are said to have been performed by Baptist ministers in dispatching great numbers of immersions in a short time, and I will not stop to question their truth. But the apostles were not working upon a wager as to time, or striving to see within how few minutes the task might be accomplished."

"No, father, and I never hear any body making such a computation without feeling shocked by it," said Mary. "When our hearts are tender and solemn at reading this wondrous work of God's grace, introducing the blessed dispensation of the Spirit, and bringing so many souls in faith and penitence to the Saviour, whom, a few days before, many of them had joined in crucifying — then, to be told of such a scene as, by the supposition, the immersion of them in some unknown, possible pool in the city, must have been, — twelve men hurrying to dispatch their two hundred and fifty a piece before dark, I feel it to be little better than profanation and mockery!"

"But the same difficulty remains on any theory," said Joseph. "Pray, Cousin Mary, how did they do it, if they sprinkled the three thousand?"

"I will answer you," said Mr. Stanley, "by reading an account of a memorable scene that actually occurred in the Sandwich Islands. 'In the afternoon of the first Sunday of July, 1838, seventeen hundred and five men, women, and children were baptized, and twenty-four hundred communicants sat down at the table of the Lord. The great crowd of people at the morning-service had been dismissed. Down through the middle of the house are seated, first, the original members of the church, perhaps fifty in number. The missionary then calls upon the head man of each village to bring forward his people. With note-book in hand, he carefully selects the converts who have been previously accepted. They have been for many weeks at the station, for instruction and examination. The multitude of candidates are then seated upon the earth floor, in close rows, with space enough between for one to walk in. There is prayer and singing, and an explanation, made many times before lest any should trust in the external rite, is given anew of the baptism they are now to receive. Then, with a basin of water in his hand, the pastor, rapidly, reverently, passes back and forth along the silent rows, and every head receives the sealing ordinance. When all have been thus touched, he advances to the front, and raising his hand, pronounces the hallowed words, "I baptize you all into the name of the Father, of the Son, and of the Holy Ghost. Amen." How impressive! How simple! How easy for one missionary, in this way, to baptize nearly two thousand in an afternoon; but how utterly impossible had he immersed them!'"

"Is it not an historical fact," said Joseph, "that upon Easter Sunday A. D. 400 Chrysostom, aided by the clergy of his own church, did immerse about three thousand catechumens at Constantinople? Also that in A. D. 496, Remigius, bishop of Rheims, immersed Clovis and three thousand of his subjects?"

"How well authenticated these 'facts' are, I do not know, but conceding them in full, there is but slight resemblance between them and the baptism at pentecost. Chrysostom was bishop of the patriarchal church at Constantinople, the imperial city of the East. The clergy of the city and suburbs who owned his supremacy numbered hundreds. Everything which wealth, aided by royal favor, could afford would be done to prepare for such an event, and the entire day may have been taken up for the purpose. So in the latter case. The baptism of a king, his courtiers and subjects, would make time, place, and circumstances wait upon its convenience. It should be added, however, that many things related of the baptism of Clovis are unworthy of credit, such as the miracles wrought on that occasion, the descent of a dove from heaven, bearing a vial of oil for his anointing, etc. (Mosheim vol. 1: p. 315).[1]

---

[1] "With respect to the baptism of Clovis and his army, the original authority is Gregory of Tours, (His. Francorum, Lib. II. chap. 31). The passage relating to the king is, 'Rex ergo prior poposcit se a pontifice baptizari,'— the king first asked to be himself baptized by the pontiff. Of the army, 'De exercitu vero ejus baptizati sunt tria

"Well, father," said Mary, "it can't be necessary to say more of this first instance of Christian baptism. It is settled by common sense. The assumption that it was by immersion need not be pronounced impossible, but it is improbable in the very highest degree. What was the next instance?"

"The baptism of *the Eunuch*, recorded in Acts 8: 26-40, which Miss Nellie will please read to us.

"There is absolutely nothing here to determine the mode in which the baptism was performed. It is simply a balance of probabilities. On the one hand is the 'water' by the roadside, but this does not imply a place large and deep enough for an immersion. Dr. Robinson found a little water 'standing along the bottom,' of a wady or valley near Tell el-Hasy which he thinks may have been the scene of the baptism. A fountain is shown about five miles from Jerusalem, and another at Bethsur near Hebron, which tradition reports as the place. But it is in the

---

millia,' — of his army three thousand were baptized. And this is all. How long it took, and how many clergymen assisted in the administration of the rite we are not informed. And the rite itself was 'baptism,' not immersion. I mean Greory of Tours can be held only for that." MS. Letter of Prof R. D. Hitchcock.

highest degree improbable that an immersion was administered *in* a fountain, both because its construction would not permit of it, and the waters would be polluted by it. The verbs 'went down' and 'came up' do not signify an *immerging* and *emerging*, but simply a descent and an ascent of the banks containing the water; and the prepositions 'into' and 'out of' might just as truly have been rendered *to* and *from*. Take this very chapter; the word *eis* — into — occurs in it eleven times; once it stands in a phrase untranslated, once it is rendered *at*, once *unto*, twice *in*, five times *to*, and only in this 38th verse *into*. Elsewhere, it occurs in the following passages. 'They repented not *at* the preaching of Jonah;' 'I will send (to) them prophets and apostles.' 'Jesus stood *on* the shore.' 'Jesus cometh *to* the grave.' 'Go thou *to* the sea and cast a hook.' 'When we were all fallen *to* the earth.' 'The other disciple did outrun Peter, and came first *to* the sepulcher — yet went he not *in*.' (John 20: 4, 5). Here it is expressly asserted that *eis* did not mean into. And we have only to substitute the word *into* in these places to see how absurd the pretense that such is its only meaning. So with the word *ek*. 'The coat was

without seam, woven *from* the top throughout.'
'The tree is known *by* its fruit.' 'Having agreed with the laborers *for* a penny.' 'Jesus knew *from* the beginning.' 'He riseth *from* supper.' 'That they may rest *from* their labors,' etc.

"But as I have remarked before, I do not care to press these critical points. I think the probabilities are, that Philip and the eunuch came to some collection of shallow waters by the wayside. I do not think there was a river or a pond, for nothing of the sort is found on the road from Jerusalem to Gaza, at present, and the way we know was 'desert' then as it is now. Dismounting from the chariot, and descending the wady, I presume they slipped off their sandals, and tucking their loose upper garments above their knees, they stepped into the edge of the water, where Philip, taking up the liquid in his hand, poured it upon the head of the officer. This would be in exact accordance with the language of the record, and with the customs prevailing through all the East to this day. I have myself often seen persons in India come to the brink of a stream or a pond, lay off their sandals, step a little way into the water, then scoop it up with their hands and drink. If fatigued and heated they unwrap, their shoulder cloth, or shawl, bind it about the waist, tuck up about the hips the cloth which is worn from the waist to the knee, wade in nearly to the hips, throw water upon their faces, shoulders, and arms, and thus refresh themselves. Ordinary bathing is done by standing in a tank or by a well, and pouring the water from a vessel over the head. Submersion is rarely if ever performed. I do not know that I ever witnessed it except in the open sea. They would consider their tanks polluted by it. Even when they wash their hands, they do it invariably by having water poured over them, never by immersing them in it."

"What do you think suggested the idea of baptism to the eunuch?" asked Arthur.

"It is impossible to say certainly. We are told that he had been up to Jerusalem to worship. While there he could hardly help hearing of the exciting events which had recently occurred, the crucifixion of Jesus, his alleged resurrection from the dead, the scenes of the day of pentecost, and the rapidly increasing number of persons who were professing faith in Jesus as the Messiah, and being baptized in his name. A deep impression seems to have been made on his mind by these things; and now having started for home, he devotes the quiet hours of his journey to a study of the prophecies relating to the coming and character of the Messiah. Just then the Evangelist, divinely directed, meets him. He is found to be reading the remarkable passage in the fifty-second and fifty-third chapters of Isaiah. Philip, at his request, explains it, and preaches to him Jesus. Whether his Septuagint copy had the words as they stand in the Hebrew, and in our English version, 'So shall he *sprinkle* many nations," etc., (ch. 52: 15) or not, is of little consequence. With an inspired commentator as his guide, he could not fail to have had a true exposition of the passage as predicting the purifying work of the Messiah, of which baptism was the appointed symbol and seal. The result of this instruction was most happy. The officer accepted this new doctrine with the docility of a child, and presently espying the water by the roadside, is ready himself to receive the rite, emblematic of the Spirit's work, that should initiate him into the visible company of the believers.

"In view of all the circumstances, I conclude that there is nothing whatever to show that there was an immersion in this case, while, on the other hand, the passage he had been reading, the teaching of Philip, the supposed location where it occurred, and the known habits of the people of the East, all concur in making it probable that it was a baptism by pouring."

"I think" said Mary, "that the next instance on record was the baptism of *Saul of Tarsus*. (Acts 9: 10-19). And I cannot see that there is any more evidence of immersion in this case, than in that of the eunuch."

"No," said Mr. Stanley, "not so much, if less than none be possible. Three days had now elapsed since the fierce young zealot had seen that overpowering vision on his way to Damascus, and during all this time, he had been totally blind, and too much agitated to eat or drink. The darkness that enshrouded his senses, and the deeper darkness of his mind, the conviction of his guilt as a persecutor of Jesus, his perplexity and despair, seem to have utterly prostrated him. While in this extremity, Ananias comes in with his message of cheer: 'Jesus, who met thee in the way, hath sent me that thou mayest receive thy sight, and be filled with the Holy Ghost.' The scales fall from his eyes, his sight is restored, he rises and is baptized forthwith. He does not go from the place; he does not wait to receive food. Just as he is, and where he is, as soon as the hands of God's messenger are laid upon him, there is poured upon him, first, the baptism of the Spirit, and next its outward token, the baptism by water. The divine affusion sheds light into his mind and peace into his heart, and now, taking the needful nourishment of which he has been so long unable to partake, he speedily regains his wonted strength.

"Dr. Carson, as usual, will not tolerate any suggestion of probabilities in this case. The word 'baptized' settles everything. As to the objection that Saul was a sick man, he says, 'I see nothing in his case to prevent his immediate immersion. I consider such reasoning as the most egregious trifling. If Paul was baptized in a state of exhaustion before partaking of refreshment, we are not from this to deny the meaning of the word, but to learn that baptism ought to be attended to immediately on believing. I care not that it was expressly said that he was baptized in the very room where he was sitting, immediately after the address of Ananias. This would not create the smallest difficulty.' (p. 356) It is fortunate, however, that Dr. C.'s assertions do not, authoritatively, settle this matter. Other people have discernment as well as he, and they will judge whether positions so extravagant are worthy of reception or not."

"The next chapter," said Arthur, "presents to us the baptism of *Cornelius*."

"Yes, and a memorable one it was, being the first instance of the baptism of a Gentile. Many of the circumstances resembled those of Saul's baptism, especially in that it was done on the spot, in the house, and was accompanied by the outpouring of the Holy Spirit. The language in which this is described is eminently suggestive. In explaining the matter to the brethren at Jerusalem, Peter said, ' As I began to speak, the Holy Ghost *fell on them* as on us at the beginning. Then remembered I the word of the Lord, how that he said, " John indeed baptized with *water*, but ye shall be baptized with the *Holy Ghost*." Forasmuch then as God gave them the like gift, as he did unto us who believed on the Lord Jesus Christ, what was I that I could withstand God?' The two baptisms are here placed in the closest connection, and the apostle says that witnessing the latter convinced him that he ought to administer the former; in other words, seeing the

Spirit *poured upon* Cornelius, he should *pour upon* him the water also."

"I notice a peculiarity of expression in the 47th verse," said Nellie, " but do not know that it has any special significance. 'Can any man forbid water that these should not be baptized,' etc. This looks as if the meaning was 'forbid water *to be brought*,' not 'forbid these to go to the water.'"

"You are right, Miss Ashton. The expression resembles that used in the case of the infants, — 'Suffer the little children to come to me, and forbid them not,' *i. e.*, to be brought. It very clearly shows that the rite was performed on the spot, with water brought in for the purpose, and that it could not therefore have been done by immersion. Dean Alford's note on this verse is very conclusive. 'The *water*, the *Spirit*, the TWO great PARTS *of full and complete baptism*, the latter infinitely greater than, but not superseding the necessity of, the former. The article here should certainly be expressed: Can any forbid *the* water to these who have received *the Spirit*? The expression *to forbid*, used with *the water*, is interesting as showing that the practice was to bring the water to the candidates, not the candidates to the water. This, which would be implied by the word under any circumstances, is rendered certain, when we remember that they were assembled *in the house.*'"

"*Lydia and her household* come next," said Arthur — " in Acts 16: 13 –15. But I see here very little to throw light upon the subject of our inquiries."

"And that very fact,"said Mary, "seems to me quite suggestive. I have been thinking how unlike all these narratives of baptisms are to what they would have been if left us by our modern Baptists. Not a single case, when carefully examined, gives a hint of any thing like an immersion. No place unmistakably capable of it is mentioned, no going out to any such place, no bringing in of a bath tub or filling it with water, no change of clothing, no preparation of any sort. On other occasions such matters are not overlooked. When Jesus was about to wash his disciples' feet, he laid aside his garments and took a towel and girded himself. When Bartimeus was called, he cast away his garment and came to Jesus. The men who stoned Stephen laid down their clothes at Saul's feet. Such items of preparation introduced into a narrative, not only enliven it, but give it naturalness and effect. But in all these immersions, as they are called, even on so remarkable an occasion as the baptism of three thousand in a single day, not a solitary glimpse of any such attending incident is left us. A remarkable fact if they *were* immersions, but very natural if they were in modes which needed no preparation."

" True," said her father, " and this is the more forcible when contrasted with the way baptisms are described in a later age, when immersion was practiced. Then much was made of the laying off of the garments. Thus ' Basil rose up with fear, *undressed himself*, putting off the old man, and went down, praying, into the water ;' " Rob. Hist. of Bap. ch. xv.

" But the *place* of baptism is mentioned often," said Joseph. " Lydia had gone out to the river side, where prayer was wont to be made ; and being converted there, was undoubtedly baptized in the river, — the Strymon, I think."

" No ; the Strymon was some distance west of the city. It was a small branch of that river, called the Gangas, or Gangitas. Prof. Hackett says that in summer, at which time this event occurred,— for they would not have resorted to that unsheltered spot for prayer in the cold season, — this stream is almost dry, (Com. p. 258.) However, nothing is said as to where she was baptized, and if it was by the river side, it may still not have been done by immersion. I cannot think it would comport with the delicacy of a Christian lady in the East, to be publicly immersed by men in a river, within or near to a great city. While there is not a shadow of evidence in support of such an idea, there is the highest improbability against it."

"Well, of that every one must judge for himself," said Joseph. "But if probabilities are to outweigh the known meaning of the word itself, we can arrive at no certain conclusion whatever. In the remaining instance recorded in the Acts. however, — that of the baptism of the *Jailer* at Philippi, — you must, I think, admit that the probabilities are on the other side."

"Will you please to mention them?" said Mr. Stanley.

"Why, it is said that the jailer brought the apostles out of the prison into his own house, and there bathed their wounds, implying of course, that he had a bath there. Then it is immediately added, 'he was baptized and all his house;'

evidently in the same bath which he had just used."

"I fear you are stating the circumstances from imperfect recollection, and not with the book before you. As to the jail, we learn from verse 24, that it consisted of two parts, an outer and an inner prison, the latter evidently a dungeon, fitted up with stocks, etc. The keeper's house, as appears from verse 34, was in an upper story of the same building, the participle — *anegagon* — being literally, having brought them *up* into his house. So Prof. Hackett renders it, adding, 'which appears to have been *over* the prison.'

"These facts show us very clearly what was done on that memorable night. First the jailer 'brought them out' of the dungeon into the outer prison. Not only is it not said that they left the house, but every thing is against that supposition. This was *before* he was converted, and before Paul had told him what to do to be saved; of course it was not done in order to be baptized, for baptism in that moment of intense alarm had not entered his thoughts. Besides, to have taken them from the prison itself, would have been to violate his duty as an officer, and expose himself to the very danger under the apprehension of which he was still trembling and ready to commit suicide, that of having permitted them to escape. For the Roman law was express, that the officer who should let an accused person escape, should himself suffer the same punishment that would have been due to him.[1] In this outer prison was doubtless the source of supply for water to the establishment. Alford suggests 'a well'; Hackett an 'impluvium,' 'a rectangular reservoir or basin for receiving the rain which flowed from the slightly inclined roof.' At this, but certainly not *in* this, he washed the apostles' bleeding wounds, which was immediately reciprocated by the baptism of himself and all his family; 'a beautiful interchange of washings,' as Bengel calls it. I say, not *in* this, — for such an act would have polluted all the water of the prison, and besides, was contrary to what we know was the constant practice of the Greeks and Romans as to the mode of bathing. Having thus performed this double washing, the jailer brings the apostles up into his own apartments, and sets food before

---

"Nam ipsum volumus hujusmodi poenæ consumi cui obnoxius docebitur fuisse qui fugerit." Wetstein in Alford's Com. on Act 16: 27.

them, after which they spend the night in rejoicing and praise to God."

"But Dr. Carson interprets the story very differently," said Joseph. "'Paul,' he says, 'preached in the jailer's house, and after the baptism, was brought back to the house, which appears to show that the baptism was at the Strymon, or some other place out of doors.'"

"Which only proves that his geography is as conjectural as his interpretation. Prof. Hackett, who has personally visited the place, expressly says that the Strymon was at 'some distance' from the city, and whether the Gangas was near enough to be accessible 'can not be decided.' That they went out of the prison at all is a mere guess, in the face of the most glaring inprobabilities. Remember that the hour was midnight; that the jailer was responsible with his life for their safe keeping; and that next day, when the magistrates offered to let them go privately, they refused, saying that they had been publicly committed and must be as publicly released. Did Paul, think you, say this while at the same time concious that the jailer and all his family, and possibly all the prisoners besides, knew that he had been clandestinely abroad during the night?"

"I think, my son," said Mrs. Mason, "that you will have to give up this case. Strongly attached as we are to our views, it does not become us to insist on improbabilities in maintaining them."

"Well, mother, if *you* give up, I don't know what will happen next. Uncle Charles has chosen his own way of discussing the subject, and has certainly succeeded in investing his positions with great plausibility. But I for one cannot go with him until he can convince me that all the learned world are wrong in the meaning they assign to *baptizo*, and its derivatives used in giving a name to this Christian sacrament."

"I trust that will come in due time," said Mr. Stanley, smiling. "Just now we are considering the question, what the apostles *did* in fulfilling their commission. We have gone with them to all the instances in which they administered baptism, so far as they are recorded, and we see the result. We fail to find a single one which was clearly and unequivocally an immersion. Yet, by the theory that such is the uniform and exclusive import of the word, we ought to have found them all such. Where, I ask, in all the range of literature, was ever such demands put forth in behalf of a word, which, in every recorded instance of actual use, it so utterly failed to substantiate?"

"We are ready now, are we not, father, for the evidence left us by the apostles of their understanding of their commission, in their *teachings* on the subject?" inquired Mary.

"Yes, and the first thing that strikes us here is to find how little prominence was given by them to the rite in any way. Only a very few times is it mentioned at all, and then only in the most casual manner. Most remarkable of all, it is never spoken of in a way that gives any certain clew to the mode in which it was to be administered. Does this look as if they regarded the mode as the very essence of the rite, so that if not done in this way, it was not done at all?"

"If I remember rightly," observed Arthur, "Paul thanks God that he had baptized none of the Corinthians but Crispus and Gaius."

"Yes," said Mary, "and the household of Stephanas; and he adds, 'For Christ sent me not to baptize, but to preach the gospel.' It is very evident that Paul was not as anxious to get people into the water as some we have seen in our day."

"And yet, it would be wrong to infer that the rite was not important, or that the Corinthians were received to the church without it. It only teaches us that we are not to exalt the rite unduly, making this, much less the *form* of it, one of the essentials of Christian faith or practice.

"The most important of the apostolic allusions to baptism, at least as estimated by the great stress put upon it by our Baptist friends, is, undoubtedly, that contained in Rom. 6: 3-6; which Miss Nellie will please read to us. A similar allusion is also found in Col. 2: 12."

She read both the passages mentioned, and Mr. S. proceeded: —

"The estimation in which these are held by Baptists is shown from the language of Dr. Carson. 'I value the evidence of these passages so highly, that I look on them as perfectly decisive. They contain God's own explanation of his own ordinance. And in this I call upon my unlearned brethren to admire the Divine wisdom. They do not understand the original; and the adoption of the words *baptize* and *baptism* can teach them nothing. But the evidence of the passages in question cannot be hid, and it is obvious to the most unlearned. The Spirit of God has, by this explanation, enabled them to judge for themselves in this matter. While the learned are fighting about *baptizo* and certain Greek prepositions, let the unlearned turn to Rom. 6: 4, and Col. 2: 12, etc.' (pp. 144, 145.) It becomes necessary, then, to examine them somewhat closely.

"' *We are buried with Christ in baptism,*' said the Apostle. Of course the figure implies that there is a *resemblance* between baptism and his burial. The point of inquiry before us is, what is that resemblance?

"Baptists say it consists in the *form* of baptism. A burial, in their view, is like immersion, in which a person is put under the water, just as one is put into a grave and covered up. 'What can be more conclusive?' they exclaim. 'Behold God's own exposition of the mode of baptism.' And ignorant and unthinking persons, not perceiving the deep spiritual meaning underlying the figure, are carried away by this superficial resemblance, which, after all, is wholly imaginary. I have no doubt that, practically, this fancy has more to do in determining men's opinions as to the form of the rite, than all other arguments together."

"What!" exclaimed Mary, "more. than the baptism *in* Jordan, and the going down *into*, and coming up *out of*, the water?"

"Yes," replied her father, "more than these; indeed, I only repeat to you what a very intelligent Baptist avowed to me not long since, as to the impression on his own mind.

"This is one of the passages in which is set before us, in a figure, the effect of the Spirit's work in the soul. As that work is symbolized by baptism, it is said to be done in or by — *dia* — baptism. We are *buried* with Christ, of course made dead to sin, by baptism.

"Now there are several other figures, no less striking, in which the same work is similarly set forth. One was that used by our Lord himself, in his conversation with Nicodemus, 'Except a man be *born* of water and of the Spirit, he cannot enter into the kingdom of God.' That reference was here made to baptism, I think, cannot be doubted; for although the Christian ordinance had not been instituted, yet John's baptism, with which Nicodemus was familiar, was of divine authority, and in its one idea of repentance, or spiritual renovation, had the same import.

"Another figure was used by the apostle in

Gal. 3: 27. 'As many of you as have been baptized into Christ, have *put on Christ*.' This passage is remarkably similar in its very language and form to the one under consideration. The figure is that of putting on a new garment in place of the old one. Elsewhere, it is 'putting off the old man, and putting on the new.'

"In Acts 22: 16, baptism is represented as a *washing*. 'Arise, and be baptized, and wash away thy sins.'

"A fourth instance is found in 1 Peter 3: 21, 'Baptism doth now save us — not the putting away of the filth of the flesh, but the *answer of a good conscience* toward God.' This expression is obscure, and commentators are not entirely agreed as to its meaning. Most suppose it is an allusion to the questions which used to be put to candidates for baptism, as to their faith and penitence, which, if they could answer with a good conscience, they were accepted. In this view, the phrase is nearly equivalent to 'professing a good profession.' 1 Tim. 6: 12.

"Still again the figure of a *resurrection* is used. Col. 2: 12. 'Baptism, wherein also ye are risen with him, through the faith of the operation of God.'

"Here, then, are no less than six different things, (and several others might be added, as being crucified, being enlightened, etc.), which we are expressly said to do in baptism. We are *born anew;* we are *washed;* we *put on a new garment;* we *put in an answer;* we are *buried;* we *rise* from the dead. We do all these in the same rite, and *do them all at once.* Now, what sort of a rite must that be which, by its form or mode, gives rise to all these dissimilar and conflicting images? one which makes us to be born when we are washed, to answer inquiries when we are buried, and to rise from the dead when we put on a garment? The very supposition is an absurdity, and shows that outward form is not to be thought of."

"But," said Joseph, "baptism may have suggested the figure of a burial, because there is a real likeness to it in an immersion, which does not exist in other cases. No form of baptism ever thought of is like a birth, or a putting on of a garment, or a rising from the dead."

"True, and immersion is as little like the entombment of Christ. Recall for a moment what that burial was:

"1. The body was closely wrapped in cloths from head to foot, inclosing aromatic drugs.

"2. It was lifted from the earth and carried into the tomb, not walking in itself, as a candidate for immersion walks into the water.

"3. The tomb was a room above ground, cut in the solid rock, similar, doubtless, to the numerous tombs still existing around Jerusalem, in which persons sometimes reside. Compare Luke 8: 27.

"4. The body was laid upon a shelf or niche.

"5. No enveloping element, whether water or earth, was permitted to come into contact with it.

"6. The body was left in the tomb, not thrust in for a moment and immediately taken out again.

"7. The entrance was closed and sealed up, that nobody might open the tomb, and remove the body.

"Now what appreciable resemblance to all this is it for a person to wade into a tank waist-deep, accompanied by another in waterproof garments to avoid being wetted, and there to have his head and shoulders dipped for a moment by the latter, beneath the water? I confess I can see very little. Say, if you please, that there is the one idea of *inness*, or putting in, common to both, yet how very far is this from determining absolutely the form of the rite, like one of the carefully framed statutes of the ancient ritual, so exactly defining and enacting it that not to do it *in this way* is not to do it at all.

"We are to seek then the source of all this imagery not in the form of the outward rite but in its *spiritual signification*. Baptism is the symbol of moral renovation by the Spirit of God. That renovation *is* a new birth, a washing, a putting on of Christ, the answer of a good conscience, a burial to sin, a resurrection. It is each and all at the same time, without confusion or contradiction. When a key fits a lock having half a dozen wards, we know it is the right key; when it fits but one of the six, we are sure it was never made for the place. This view, and this alone, harmonizes with the apostle's reasoning here. An objector to his doctrine of justification by grace says, it is an encouragement to sin. 'No,' says Paul, 'it is not, for a baptized person is dead to sin; nay, more, he is buried in the tomb with his Lord, and is no longer susceptible to its power. Henceforth, his life is hid with Christ in God.' This is good reasoning, if the baptism he means is the real work of the Spirit in the soul. But if it be the outward rite, an immersion, the reasoning would be, 'No, it is not an encouragement to sin, for the man has been into the baptistery!'

"Observe further, that apart from these two passages, baptism is never either in the Old Testament or the New made a symbol of death or of burial, but universally of *purification*. Death was to a Jewish mind always associated with impurity. A dead body was unclean; a grave a place of corruption. To have made baptism symbolical of either would have been to render it the most repulsive thing possible. But the complex spiritual idea of *dying with Christ*, and of being *dead to sin*, was the idea of purification; of getting rid of the old corrupt man and all its pollution, and entering upon a new life of holiness; and this is just what baptism as a rite of *cleansing* is fitted to signify. There are but two sacraments under the Christian dispensation, the Lord's Supper and baptism. The former represents the death of Christ; why should the other do the same? And if both are emblematic of his death and burial, where is the rite which shows the Spirit's work?

"On this point, the remarks of Prof. Stuart are very weighty. 'Under the ancient dispensation,' says he, 'the rites were divided into two great classes, viz., those significant of *purity or purification*, and those significant of *atonement for sin*. Nothing could be more appropriate than this. Man needed the one and the other, in order to find acceptance with God; the one is the work of the Spirit, and the other of the Saviour, who redeemed us by his blood. Is there any change in the *essential* conditions of salvation under the new dispensation? None, we must answer. Are not the significant symbols, then, under the new dispensation, a summary of those which existed under the old? The belief of this spontaneously forces itself upon my mind. The work of the Spirit is still symbolized under the gospel, and a Saviour's blood is still represented. The one baptism signifies; the other is as plainly indicated by the Lord's Supper.'" Am. Bib. Rep. Vol. 3. p. 269.

"Oh! Mr. Stanley," said Nellie, "you have destroyed one of the most affecting aspects of this sacrament to me. I have often heard of being 'buried with Christ in baptism,' and have always supposed the phrase had reference to this rite. I have seen ministers lead happy converts down into what they called 'the liquid grave,' and as they came up have heard them sing:

> 'Thou hast said, exalted Jesus,
>   "Take thy cross and follow me:'
> Shall thy word with terror seize us,
>   Shall we from the burden flee?
>   Lord I'll take it,
>   And, rejoicing, follow thee.
>
> 'While this liquid tomb surveying,
>   Emblem of my Saviour's grave,
> Shall I shun its brink, betraying
>   Feelings worthy of a slave?
>   No. I'll enter;
>   Jesus entered Jordan's wave.
>
> 'Should it rend some fond connection,
>   Should I suffer shame or loss,
> Yet the fragrant, blest reflection,
>   I have been where Jesus was,
>   Will revive me,
>   When I faint beneath the cross.'

"Now is all this a mistake? Do not persons in their baptism follow Christ into the grave, and from it rise again with him to a new life of holiness?"

"I answer you," said Mr. Stanley, "by returning your own questions. *Do* persons, in the outward rite of baptism, immersion — in a baptistery, if you please, — become dead to sin, and *are* they then really buried with Christ? Has not the baptism which effects *that*, the work of the Holy Ghost, taken place previously? Is it not one of the fundamental principles of the Baptists that only believers, — that is renewed or spiritually baptized persons, — are to be admitted to baptism? That death to sin *has been* experienced, — it is a thing of the past, already having evidenced itself by confession and fruits meet for repentance. Cornelius was buried with Christ in baptism when the Holy Ghost *fell upon* him. Suppose that he never received the outward rite, that fact would have remained all the same. All truly regenerated souls are in this respect alike, whether they ever receive water-baptism or not. Even we Pedobaptists, who have only been sprinkled, are, so far, precisely on the same footing with Baptists themselves. It is not denied that we are Christians, regenerated by the Spirit, the only baptism that makes dead to sin and entombs with Christ. When, therefore, they tell us that we have not been baptized, because not immersed, and yet admit that we have had the baptism in which souls are buried with Jesus, it is only the same thing as saying that that baptism is not immersion.

"Besides, if you take the opposite view, you have, in its most repulsive form, baptismal regeneration. If we are buried with Christ in *immersion*, then immersion becomes a saving ordinance. Not tender, helpless babes—for they are never permitted to come to this rite—but adults of every age, have only to go into the baptistery to become dead to sin, and alive to God through Jesus Christ!"

"But uncle," said Joseph, "you do not surely intend to charge such a doctrine as that upon us. We do not pretend that in immersion we are actually buried with Christ, but only symbolically so; and from the thing symbolized, we think we are instructed what the form of the symbol should be."

"Yes, but you deny us the right to reason in the same way. We hold that baptism is a symbol of 'the washing of regeneration, and renewing of the Holy Ghost, *which he shed on us* abundantly through Jesus Christ,' (Tit. 3: 5, 6.), and we think that the thing symbolized teaches us what the form of the symbol should be. We think, too, that ours is the more perfect symbol, because it is a real pouring, whereas immersion is not a real burial, nor even a resemblance to one, unless it be a burial in the sea. It certainly was not like the tearful laying away of the sacred body of Jesus in the virgin tomb of Joseph.

"The truth is that baptism, whatever its mode, is an emblem of a spiritual operation, which strictly speaking has no form. That operation is imaged to us in a great many ways. Now there is no objection to making the form of our outward symbol, water-baptism, like any one of these. We think the sprinkling or pouring appropriate, — you immersion. We find the likeness in one mode, you in another. There is no harm in this so long as neither of us insist that ours is the only permissible one, and do not excommunicate each other for using, in this respect, the liberty with which Christ hath made us free.

"Our next important allusion in the teaching of the apostles to the subject of baptism, is in 1 Cor. 10 : 1-2. 'All our fathers were under the cloud, and all passed through the sea, and were all *baptized unto Moses* in the cloud and in the sea.'"

"This is one of the passages," said Joseph, "which we claim as teaching immersion."

"How do you make that out?" said Mary.

"Surely, the only persons immersed on that occasion were the Egyptians."

"The Hebrews were at least surrounded by water. The cloud was above them, and the sea standing in lofty walls on either side. Besides, it is expressly said they were baptized *in* the cloud and *in* the sea."

"But the cloud," said Mr. Stanley, "was not a watery cloud. It was the supernatural symbol of God's presence, — the Shechinah, which at night was a pillar of fire. Neither were they *under* it in a local sense, but simply under its guidance and protection. Locally, it was *before* them until they began the passage of the sea, when it withdrew and took its position *behind* them. As to the sea-walls, they must have been far apart — probably several miles; for it can be demonstrated that nothing less than such a space would have been sufficient for the passage of three millions of people, with immense flocks and herds, in a single night. Underneath them was dry ground. Nothing like *envelopment* then, by the cloud or by the sea, can be imagined here. We must not make Paul's account contradict that of Moses. The Greek word *en*, as we have seen before, very often means *by*, denoting the instrumental agent. They were baptized *by* the cloud and the sea, *i. e.* by the Shechinah of the Divine Presence, and the miracle of the divided waters. Such an amazing interposition in their behalf was like a sacramental oath, consecrating them to Moses as God's vicegerent, and solemnly binding them to his service.

"In this case then there was no outward rite whatever. It was a purely *ideal* baptism, called such not because of any form, for there was none, but because of its effect. The miracle bound the nation to Moses, as Christians are consecrated by their baptism to Christ. It was to them what that is to us, just as the manna and the waters of the rock were to them what the Lord's supper is to us. The design of the apostle was to show that the Jewish people constituted a church, with its two sacraments, and were therein a type of the Christian church and its sacraments."

"The next passage in order," said Arthur, "is 1 Cor. 12: 13. '*For by one Spirit are we all baptized into one body*, whether we be Jews or Gentiles, whether we be bond or free; and have been all made to drink into one Spirit.'"

"It is important to us in this discussion," said

his father, "as showing that the baptism of the Holy Spirit, represented to us so constantly under the image of a pouring out, is experienced by all Christians, and was not confined to what might be regarded as the special occasions when miraculous gifts were conferred, as in the case of Christ and his apostles, and others in the primitive church. And this shows us, too, what kind of baptism the apostle referred to when he spoke of being buried with Christ. All true believers *have* this baptism, all are by it made dead to sin, which is not true of the outward rite. How plainly, therefore, is the reference to the former and not to the latter."

"In Ephesians 4: 5, we have the expression, 'One Lord, one faith, *one baptism*,'" said Mary, "but I do not know that this will help us any in respect to the subject of inquiry."

"A short time since," said Arthur, "I heard a Baptist minister, on reading this text, remark, 'There, you see, Paul declares there is only one *way* of baptism, and he certainly knew.'"

"Of course," replied his father, "he presumed on the ignorance of his auditors. The connection of the verse shows that no reference at all was intended to the mode of baptism. Paul was making an appeal for Christian unity—such a one as I could wish were made anew to us all at the present day—from the oneness of the Christian system, in which all true disciples are embraced. 'We have,' says he, 'one Lord, one faith, one baptism,' *i. e.* one ordinance of consecration to him. Nobody pretends that we and our brethren have different baptisms. We alike profess to believe in and to practice that *one* baptism which Christ has appointed. The only question is *how* we shall do it. An argument from this expression for one *mode* alone, can excite only our pity at the ignorance or the disingenuousness of him who uses it."

"The passage in 1 Peter 3: 20, 21," said Nellie, "you have already referred to, but did not explain the allusion contained in it to the baptism of Noah and his family in the waters of the flood."

"No such baptism is asserted of them," replied Mr. Stanley, "either here or elsewhere. It is simply said that Noah and his family—eight souls in all—were *saved* by water. That is, the water buoying up the ark with its inmates, saved them from the destruction which came upon the rest of mankind. It is not said that they were baptized either in the water or in the ark. But the mention of *water* as the instrument of saving the patriarch, suggests to him Christian baptism, which he says 'doth also now save us,'—*i. e.* of course, meaning that spiritual renovation of which baptism is the emblem."

"But," said Joseph, "the apostle asserts that baptism was 'a like figure unto' the deluge; which certainly was an immersion on the grandest scale, covering the whole world and all its inhabitants except the family of Noah."

"An unfortunate proof text, I think, for the immersionists, for the only persons really immersed at that time were the impenitent. It is a curious and amusing specimen of persistency in pushing a theory beyond the bounds of reason or sense, that is exhibited by Carson, in maintaining that Noah and his family were saved *by immersion* in the waters of the deluge. 'The ordinance of baptism,' says he, 'and the salvation of Noah by water, have the most lively resemblance. Noah and his family were saved *by being buried in the water of the flood;* and after the flood, they emerged as rising from the grave.' (p. 462.) 'What could be a more expressive burial in water than to be in the ark, when it was floating? As well might it be said that a person is not buried in earth when lying in his coffin covered with earth. May not persons in a ship be said figuratively to be buried in the sea? They who were in the ark were deeply immersed.' (p. 413.) And because the venerable Dr. Miller cannot see the immersion here, Dr. Carson scolds at him in this fashion. 'With as great propriety, the learned gentleman may deny that a man in a tomb is buried, because he is covered with a coffin. What! Noah not immersed *when buried in the waters of the flood?* Are there no bounds to perverseness? Will men say everything rather than admit the mode of an ordinance of Christ, which is contrary to the commandments of men?'" (p. 388.)

"What then is the meaning of the expression, 'the like figure whereunto?'" asked Joseph.

"That expression is a paraphrase rather than a translation of the original. Literally it would read 'water, which, an *antitype — antitupon* — also now saves us.' That is, water, the 'corresponding particular,' as Alford explains it, to that which saved Noah, now saves us also. That correspondence is solely in the fact that it was the *same element* in both cases. There is no reference to the quantity or mode of action in either case; indeed, the passage as a whole, has not the remotest bearing upon the subject now under consideration.

"The next passage," continued Mr. Stanley, "that calls for our consideration, is in Heb. 9: 10."

Miss Ashton read the passage, adding, "I do not see any allusion to baptism here."

"You will in a moment," he replied. "The apostle was contrasting the rites of the ceremonial law, as a means of purifying the soul, with the blood of Christ which was shed once for all. These rites, he says, consisted only of 'meats and drinks and divers washings and carnal ordinances imposed on them until the time of reformation.' The word 'washings' is in the original, *baptisms;* carnal ordinances are literally *ordinances of the flesh*, that is, which pertain to the body only in contrast with the expiatory blood of Jesus, which is applied to the heart. The more exact sense of the passage then is this; — 'meats and drinks and various *baptisms*, ordinances pertaining to the external man, imposed by the law until the time of the readjustment of things under the Messiah.'

"Now if we turn to the ancient law to seek for these ordinances, we shall find that they prescribed numerous ceremonies in which a fluid was used, as blood, or oil, or water, or water mixed with the ashes of a heifer, to signify the idea of purification. These rites were of various kinds, as applied to different persons, and on different occasions, but there was one fact of great significance common to them all, viz., that with a single exception in a peculiar case, *there was never an immersion among them all.* This fact we have before noted in our consideration of John's baptism, but it needs to be distinctly repeated here. Yet the one Greek word selected by the apostle to designate them comprehensively, is BAPTISMS. Probably the same thing is alluded to in Heb. 6: 2, where Paul speaks of the 'doctrine of baptisms,' as among the elementary things which Christians should leave behind, and pass on to the higher matters pertaining to a spiritual manhood.[1]

"Let me repeat also what was before said as

---

[1] "It includes in the idea those various washings which were under the law, the baptism of John, and even Christian baptism also perhaps included, the nature of which, and their distinctions from one another, would naturally be one of the fundamental and primary objects of teaching to Hebrew converts." Alford, Comm. in loc.

to the actual practice of the Hebrews. It is, certainly, very possible, in such a climate as that of Arabia and Palestine, that some of the numerous washings required were performed at pools or rivulets, whenever such collections of water were accessible. Persons may have bathed themselves, and cleansed their garments in the streams. But this was no part of the law; and as a general rule must have been impracticable. During forty years the Hebrews were in the desert, where running water was rarely to be found, and even fountains and wells often failed to afford a sufficiency for drinking. Look, then, at the laws requiring ablution as contained in the 14th, 15th and 16th chapters of Leviticus, and the 19th of Numbers, and see how frequently and by what vast numbers of persons it must have been performed, and you cannot escape the conviction that it was not and could not have been always done by immersion, and that it would be in the highest degree unreasonable so to interpret the law as to make it obligatory.

"Nay, the apostle himself expressly specifies some of these 'baptisms' in this very chapter. They were 'the blood of bulls and of goats, and the ashes of a heifer sprinkling the unclean.'

'And almost all things are, by the law, purged by blood, and, without shedding of blood, is no remission.' 'It was therefore necessary,' he says, 'that the patterns,' or types, 'of things in the heavens should be purified with these,' viz., sprinklings or baptisms. In contrast with which, he sets forth the vital efficacy of the blood of Christ, and adds the exhortation, 'Let us draw near with a true heart, in full assurance of faith, having our hearts *sprinkled* from an evil conscience, and our bodies *washed* with pure water.' Surely it cannot be possible to mistake the allusion here to the one efficacious Christian baptism, by the blood of Christ and the water which symbolizes it, in contrast with all those ritual baptisms of the old law which could not effect internal purification. And just as little possible for a candid mind is it to mistake the form, viz., *sprinkling*, under which both kinds of baptisms are set forth."

"This view of the matter," said Arthur, "is certainly very forcible. But the argument is wholly lost to ordinary readers of the Scriptures, inasmuch as the word used in the tenth verse is 'washings' and not 'baptisms.' It is a pity that our translators did not transfer the original word, as in other cases, rather than give us this comparatively unmeaning substitute for it."

"So I think," said Mary. "We should not, in that case, have been so often asked for examples of a sprinkling-baptism in the Scriptures."

"There is one passage more," proceeded Mr. Stanley, "which I wish to notice in this connection. "It occurs in 1 John, 5: 8. 'There are three that bear witness, [in earth[1]] the Spirit, and the water, and the blood, and these three agree in one.'"

"Does this passage allude to baptism?" asked Nellie.

"I think it does, and in a very interesting manner. The apostle is referring to the proof that Jesus is the Son of God, and that we have eternal life in him. To this fact, he says there are three witnesses. Opinions differ as to what precisely are intended by these. Dean Alford's view, I think, is the best. The *Spirit* is the Holy Spirit, 'who testifies of Christ (John 15: 26), who glorifies him, and shows of the things which belong to him, (John 16: 14).' The *water* is 'the baptism of water which the Lord himself

---

[1] It is now conceded by nearly all scholars that these words, as well as the entire seventh verse are spurious.

underwent, and instituted for his followers.' The *blood*, 'the baptism of blood which he himself underwent, and instituted for his followers.' Now we know in what way two, at least, of these witnesses gave their testimony. The Spirit was *poured out;* the blood was *shed;* did the third testify in a different way?

"I do not claim that this peculiar utterance of the apostle is a demonstration of the matter before us, but it is certainly suggestive, and very interesting. It is one of the incidental allusions which show how this Christian rite was associated in his mind, and which are conceded to be often more convincing than elaborate argument. The three witnesses are the *three baptisms* in which the believer has a common experience with his Lord, 'and these three *agree in one.*'

"We will now conclude our conversation for this time, and resume it, if you please, next Monday evening. It will not be convenient for me to meet you again sooner."

CHAPTER V.

CLASSIC USAGE.

IT was very manifest that the discussions of the previous evenings had not been without their effect on the minds of those who had engaged in them. That Arthur and Mary should be confirmed in the views in which they had been trained, was a matter of course. Even Joseph Mason had lost something of the confidence with which he had entered into the proposed plan of study. The unusual course of the discussion adopted by Mr. Stanley had embarrassed him, depriving him, as he said, of the potent argument which Baptists had been wont to derive from the alleged classic use of the words *baptizo* and *baptisma*, and which has far too generally been conceded to them, as favoring the exclusive sense of immersion. And yet he could not deny that his uncle's course was a reasonable one. As a lawyer, called to an investigation of an ancient statute, he must seek for the interpretation of that statute in contemporary facts, — the circumstances in which it was enacted, the objects to be secured by it, the known sentiments and usage of the author of the law, his attendants, and ministers. Other considerations derived from literary peculiarities, and the usages of foreign nations, of different culture, institutions and religion, must be held secondary in importance to these. Thus viewed, he could not but perceive that the argument went nearly all one way, and if he had not defended his own ground more fully and strenuously, it was, chiefly, as his cousin Mary had sportively hinted, because he found but little to say. Miss Ashton was reserved in the expression of her feelings, but was, nevertheless, working out to clear convictions on the subject. Her thoughts were not so much engrossed with the exclusive claims of the Baptists, as with the question what she should do if Joseph should persist in them, and should finally urge compliance with them upon her. However, she resolved to wait patiently the issue, committing herself silently, meanwhile, to the care of

Him who knew her heart, and had promised to his disciples the Comforter, who should guide them into all truth. Mrs. Mason was, probably, of all the party, the least impressed by what had been said. She was a Baptist from the force of circumstances, and not from an independent investigation of the subject, and, of course, was less susceptible to conviction from the side of such an investigation than from any other.

On the return of the evening designated, our friends took their places, as before, round the table of Mrs. Mason, and resumed the discussion.

"We have now," said Mr. Stanley, " finished our examination of the *Scripture* evidence, bearing upon the subject before us. We have seen what means the apostles had for understanding Christ, in the commission he gave them, — from their personal knowledge of the rite, from the use of *baptizo* and kindred words in the ancient Scriptures, from the customary speech of the Jewish people at that time, including our Lord himself, and from the higher baptism of the Holy Spirit, of which this rite was to be the symbol. Then we saw what they *did*, when they actually administered baptism, looking at all the recorded cases in the New Testament. And lastly, we examined what they *said and taught* in their own preaching and writings. From all which, we gather the following conclusions:

"1. That they understood baptism to be a rite of *purification*, symbolical of the work of the Holy Spirit in regenerating the soul, to be administered by the application of water to the person, in which he is consecrated to the service of the Father, the Son, and the Holy Ghost.

"2. That the *mode* of applying this water is not prescribed, the word itself being a *generic* term denoting purification, and not limiting the act to any mode.

"3. That the scriptual *pattern* of that method was twofold, one, conformable to the Jewish mode of ritual cleansing, by *sprinkling*, the other, derived from the higher baptism of the Holy Spirit, by *pouring;* both, however, as symbolizing the same thing, equivalent to each other, and interchangeable at pleasure.

"And now I appeal to you all, not even excepting Aunt Emily and Cousin Joseph, whether, taking the Scriptures alone for our authority, these are not fair conclusions. Could you, Joseph, as a lawyer, called to investigate an ancient document and decide upon its own proper teaching, aided, of course, by what is known of the habits, opinions, and circumstances of the people among whom it originated, come to any other result?"

"Perhaps not, replied Joseph, "with the field of inquiry thus limited. But you have as yet excluded what we regard as the most important part of that field, viz., that of *classic usage*."

"Well, I am ready now to enter that part of it with you, if you desire. But first, let us see clearly what we are to go there for."

"Why, of course, to ascertain how the native Greek or classic writers understood the word *baptizo*."

"Well, to what end?"

"If it is thus proved that they used it always and only in the sense of to immerse, then we have established the very strong presumption that Christ would use it in the same sense."

"A presumption that he *would*, perhaps, but not the fact that he *did*. What the *fact* was, we have already ascertained in another way, and no presumption can alter that. It might show that he ought to have so used it, if he would have the reputation of using pure Greek, but I do not know that he ever aspired to that. He spoke to be *understood* by his followers; we cannot doubt that he was understood; and we have seen what that understanding was. If all the native Greeks from Inachus down, poets, historians, rhetoricians, and orators, had always used the word otherwise, it would not alter his meaning. It is that, and that only, which is law to us."

"You seem to imply, sir," said Joseph, "that our Saviour spoke a different language from that of the native Greeks."

"So he did, in some important respects; indeed, so great is this difference that it has been called the 'Greek of the Synagogue,' to distinguish it from that of the classic writers. We have Lexicons peculiar to each, and if we should read the New Testament by the classic Lexicons alone, or the classics by the N. T. Lexicons, we should make each say very often what would have no truth or sense.

"For the explanation of this important fact, let me refer you to some historical statements. Greek was introduced into Asia with the invasion of Alexander, B. C. 334-323, and being the language of the conquerors and their successors, became in one or two hundred years the prevailing tongue in the East. At this time Hebrew had ceased to be spoken, having never recovered from the blow given to the nation by the captivity in Babylon. When, therefore, the Jews sought to diffuse a knowledge of their Scriptures and religion among their own people and others, they were almost shut up to the necessity of making the Greek language the instrument for so doing. The Scriptures were translated into it at Alexandria, by the Seventy, about B. C. 280. We need, then, only to remember that the Jews, as related to the Greek, were foreigners, or *barbarians*, as a Greek scholar would have termed them, whose vernacular in its structure and genius had scarcely a trace of affinity with it, and that they were in every way pre-eminently a 'peculiar people,' to see that the language, in their use of it, would inevitably be subjected to important modifications. Perhaps no two races were ever more unlike in their history, their religion and philosophy, their education and law and politics, their manners and customs, every thing, in short, that needed or was accustomed to find expression in words, than the Hellenistic tribes that inhabited the shores and isles of the Ægean, and the Hebraistic tribes that dwelt on the sacred soil of Palestine. And, certainly, no language was ever subjected to such a *strain*, if I may use the word, as that of the former, with all its copiousness and flexibility, when it was thus taken to be the vehicle for expressing, not only to the Jews themselves, but, through the New Testament, to all the world, in all time, the peculiar conceptions and teachings of the latter.

"A few examples will serve to illustrate these statements. Take, then, the greatest, in the Jewish estimation, of all words — the sacred and incommunicable name, JEHOVAH; what could they find in the language of the heathen Greeks to represent it? The nearest word was *Kurios*, meaning an owner or proprietor, the lord of an estate. Or take the word GOD, denoting the infinite Deity; they could find nothing better as its counterpart than *Theos*, literally a *Runner*, because the sun, moon, and planets, the greater divinities of the Greeks, moved or *ran across* the heavens, in their daily circuits.[1] If you should have asked a heathen Greek what Paul meant in 1 Cor. 8: 6, 'To us there is one Theos;' he might have pointed you to Zeus, his greatest

---

[1] Donnegan's Lex. Others derive it from *tithemi*, to set or fix; i. e. one who establishes; and others from the Sanscrit *Deva*, god.

god, who lived on Mt. Olympus, eating and drinking ambrosia and nectar, the husband of a *Thea* named Hera, or Juno, with whom he was almost perpetually quarreling on account of his adulteries, and lies, and disgraceful tricks, and say, 'I suppose Paul means that you Christians worship but *one* such being, while we worship millions of them.' Take the words for righteousness, sin, holiness, faith, love, heaven, spirit,[1] resurrection, and a thousand more, and he would as little know what, in their new use, they signified. So with Christ, the word, the church, min-

---

[1] Dr. Edwin Hall relates the following incident.

"Some years since I met with a man who was liberally educated, a thorough scholar, an able lawyer, and possessed of splendid natural abilities, but skeptical in his views of religion. With this man I undertook to reason of the necessity of being born of the Holy Ghost. Now the word in the Greek Testament for ghost, or spirit, is *pneuma*, which, originally, and in the classic Greek most commonly meant *wind*. This man would have me argue by book. He then turned to the Greek Testament, (John 3: 5). 'See here,' says he, 'it reads, and you know it reads, "Verily, verily, I say unto thee, except a man be born of water and of *wind*, he cannot enter into the kingdom of God." What right' said he, 'have you to change the original, classic meaning of *pneuma*, wind, here, any more than you have of *hudatos*, water? And see further,' said he, 'there is the same word in the eighth verse, letter for letter, and there you do not say, "The Spirit bloweth where it listeth;" you say, "The *wind* bloweth where it listeth."' He was right in the original, classic use of the word. And if I had argued on the principles on which our Baptist brethren have argued, I should have been obliged to allow that the renewing by the Spirit of God, or even the personal existence of such a Spirit, is not taught or referred to in this passage." Mode of Baptism pp. 15, 16.

ister, deacon, the Bible, the supper, etc. So too with the word *baptism*. These all express ideas which the heathen had never heard of, and of course implied uses which he never made of them. Shall we go to him to tell us what they must mean; and then turn out of our Christian fellowship all who will not take his explanation of them, as the very truth as it is in Jesus?"

"These statements are very strong, father," said Mary, "and if they may be taken in their full force, they must carry great weight with them. Can you quote authorities to substantiate them?"

"Certainly, my daughter, nearly every scholar who has written on the subject. Here is what Dr. George Campbell of Scotland says,—

"'With the greatest justice, it is denominated a peculiar idiom, being not only Hebrew and Chaldaic phrases put in Greek words, but even single Greek words used in senses in which they never occur in the writings of profane authors. . . . Classical use, both in the Greek and in the Latin, is not only in this study sometimes unavailable, but may even mislead. The sacred use and the classical are often very different.' Prelim. Diss. vol. 1: pp. 32, 58.

"Here, likewise, is the testimony of Prof. Ernesti, of Germany, one of the first critics and scholars of the last century: —

"'We deny without hesitation that the diction of the New Testament is pure Greek, and contend that it is modeled after the Hebrew, not only in single words, phrases, and figures of speech, but in the general texture of the language. — Nay, many parts of the New Testament can be explained in no other way than by means of the Hebrew. Moreover, in many passages, there would arise an absurd and ridiculous meaning, if they should be interpreted according to a pure Greek idiom.' pp. 56, 57.

"Similar to these is the language of Prof. Stuart: —

"Classical usage can never be very certain in respect to the meaning of a word in the New Testament. Who does not know that a multitude of Greek words have received their coloring and particular meaning from the Hebrew and not from the Greek classics? How then can you be over confident in the application of the classical meaning of *baptizo*, when the word is employed in relation to a rite that is purely Christian?'

"Prof. Geo. H. Whittemore, in the Baptist

Quarterly for Jan., 1874, says, 'There is another, the Christian element of the New Testament Greek. If we might reasonably look for the impress of nationality upon the writings composed in it, equally might be anticipated an influence from the world of new conceptions and revelations with which these words abound. As one has said, "The new life of Christianity has formed for itself a language, to give adequate expression to the thoughts and aspirations it has awakened." There is a pleasing analogy between the effect of this fresh, divine energy infused into man through the grace of Christ, seizing, animating, and amplifying the same faculties before possessed, and the new and extended import of many long established Greek words in their Christian sense. With a general meaning, obvious from their ordinary employment, the connection in which they came to be used, inevitably gave them a fuller, sometimes a unique meaning. Like the emblems and shadows of the old dispensation, the force and beauty of which could only be fully realized in the consummation of that which they prefigured, so words were informed with a new significance in the light of the great subjects on which they were employed by the sacred writers.'

"It is then more for a philological than for a doctrinal purpose that we go to classic authors to inquire for their use of the word *baptizo*. We feel very little concern as to the verdict they shall render. Perhaps, considering the utter strangeness of the *thing* meant from any thing embraced within their knowledge or conceptions, we ought to expect but very little agreement between their use of it and that of the New Testament. But whether much or little, it will in no degree affect the conclusions we have come to from the Scriptures themselves. 'To the law and to the testimony; if they speak not according to this word it is because there is no light in them.'" Isa. 8 : 20.

"I am afraid, Nellie," said Mrs. Mason, "that we women shall not be much edified by this part of the discussion."

"No," said Nellie, "it will doubtless be all *Greek* to us; however, I shall be much interested to hear it, and I hope we can gain at least something from it."

"We will do our best to make the matter intelligible even to those who do not understand the Greek themselves," said Mr. Stanley. "The points involved are not very obscure, and here as well as throughout our discussion, I wish to rely upon the common sense of candid people, rather than the profoundest learning where there is prejudice."

"That is a compliment to us," cried Mary, "in return for which we must be very good and attentive."

"There are two Greek words," said Mr. S., "whose meaning is discussed in this connection, BAPTO and BAPTIZO. Only the latter, however, and its derivatives, are used in reference to the Christian ordinance. Bapto is the primitive or root-word, and baptizo is derived from it.

"Here, in the first place, is a concise summary of the *definitions* of these words, as given by a large number of the standard Greek Lexicographers. I have copied them mostly from Dr. Rice, as adduced in his great debate with Rev. Alexander Campbell.

BAPTO.

"Hedericus defines bapto thus:—'Mergo, immergo; 2, tingo, intingo; 3, lavo,' *i. e.* to immerse, to plunge, to dye, to wash.

Scapula,—'Mergo, immergo—item tingo—inficere, imbuere—item lavo'; *i. e.* to merge, immerse; also to plunge; also to stain, dye, color; also to wash.

Coulon,—' Mergo, tingo, abluo '; *i. e.* to immerse, to dye, to cleanse.

Ursinus,—'To dip, to dye, to sprinkle, to wash.'

Schrevelius,—'Mergo, intingo, lavo, haurio˙, *i. e.* to dip, to dye, to wash, to draw water.

Groves,—'To dip, plunge, immerse, to wash, to wet, moisten, sprinkle, to steep, imbue, to dye, &c.'

Donnegan,—' To dip, to plunge into water, to submerge, to wash, to dye, to color.'

Robinson,—' To dip in, to immerse, to tinge, to dye.'

BAPTIZO.

" 'Scapula defines it thus: —'Mergo, seu immergo; item tingo; ut quae tingendi aut abluendi gratia aqua immergimus—item mergo, submergo, obruo aqua; item abluo, lavo,' (Mark 7; Luke 11), *i. e.* to dip or immerse; also to dye, as we immerse things for the purpose of coloring or washing them; also to plunge, submerge, to cover with water; also to cleanse, to wash. (Mark 7, Luke 11). *Baptismos* he thus defines: ' Mersio, lotio, ablutio, ipse immergendi, item lavandi seu abluendi actus,' (Mark vii, &c.) *i. e.* immersion, washing, cleansing, the act itself of immersing; also of washing or cleansing. (Mark 7. &c.)

Hedericus, — 'Mergo, immergo, aqua obruo. 2. abluo lavo. 3. baptizo, significatu sacro' — *i. e.* to dip, to immerse, to cover with water. 2. to cleanse, to wash. 3. to baptize, in a sacred sense.

Stephanus,—' Mergo, seu immergo, ut quae tingendi aut abluendi gratia aqua immergimus — mergo, submergo, obruo aqua, abluo, lavo,' *i. e.* to dip, to immerse, as we immerse things for the purpose of coloring or washing; to merge, submerge, to cover with water; to cleanse, to wash.

Schleusner, — Not only to plunge, immerse, but ' to cleanse, wash, purify with water.'

Parkhurst, — 'To immerse in, or wash with, water in token of purification.'

Schrevelius,—'Mergo, obluo, lavo'—*i. e.* to immerse, to cleanse, to wash.

Groves, — ' To dip, to immerse, to immerge, to plunge, to wash, to cleanse, to purify — *Baptizomai*, to wash one's self, to bathe, &c.'

Bretschneider,—' Proprie sepius intingo, sepius lavo; deinde lavo, abluo simpliciter — medium

&c.; lavo me, abluo me', *i. e.* properly often to dip, often to wash; then simply to wash, to cleanse; in the middle voice, I wash or cleanse myself.

Suidas, — Not only to sink, to plunge, to immerse, but to wet, to wash, to cleanse, to purify; (madefacio, lavo, abluo, purgo, mundo.)

Wahl, — 'To wash, to perform ablution, to cleanse; 2. to immerse', &c.

Passow, — 'Abluo and lavo,' *i. e.* to wash, to bathe.

Stokius, — ' To immerse, to wash.'

Robinson, — ' To immerse, to sink; to wash, to cleanse by washing; to baptize, to administer the rite of baptism.'

"Let it be borne in mind, as you examine this list, that the question is whether immerse is the *exclusive* meaning of these words. Baptists often quote authorities to show that it is *one* of their meanings, but this no one denies. Is it their sole meaning, as Carson, Conant, and others so positively affirm?"

"Plainly that is not the case," said Joseph. "But, after all, the definitions lexicographers give are only their opinions as to the meaning of the words, derived from their study of the authors who used them. The only certain way of determining them is to go to those authors for ourselves."

"Well, I think you are right in that; so I propose, next, to do that very thing. Let us then ask the classic writers themselves what they meant.

"The original and primary meaning of bapto is doubtless to *dip*. As to this fact, there is no dispute, and no need of quoting any authority to prove it.

"Besides this primary meaning, bapto has secondary ones denoting the *effects* of dipping, and these vary according to the nature of those effects. One of these is to *color* or *dye*, and that too, whether it be done by dipping, pouring, or even sprinkling. Thus Æschylus says, 'This garment *stained* by the sword of Ægisthus is a witness to me.' Homer, in his mock-heroic poem of the battle of the frogs and the mice, says, 'He fell and breathed no more, and the lake was tinged — *ebapteto* — with the purple blood.' Aristophanes speaks of a person who had stained — *baptomenos* — his face with tawny washes. Hippocrates says of a certain liquid,

'When it drops upon the garments they are stained,' *baptetai.* To this meaning of the word, doubtless, is to be referred the use of it in Rev. 19: 13, 'He was clothed with a vesture dipped in blood,' *i. e.* stained by the blood spirting from the wounds of his enemies. This figure we find in Isaiah 63: 3, where in the same character the Messiah says, 'Their blood shall be sprinkled on my garments, and I will stain all my raiment.'

"Another secondary sense is to smear, or spread over. Thus Sophocles says 'Thou hast well smeared — *ebapsas* — thy sword with the Grecian army,' *i. e.* with the blood of the army. Æschylus speaks of 'bathing — *bapsasa* — the sword by slaughter,' and Aristophanes, of a person 'smearing himself — *baptomenos* — with frog-colored paints,' etc.

"This secondary import of *bapto* was long denied, and it was insisted that the word meant to dip, wherever it occurred. Wonders of ingenuity were expended in showing how a garment was dipped into a sword, how a lake was dipped into the blood of a mouse, a man's face dipped into washes, etc. Even poor Nebuchadnezzar, in the Septuagint, (Dan. 5: 21), was dipped into the dew. But more sensible views have of late prevailed, possibly, because it has been remembered that this word never denotes baptism, and the concession can be safely made. Dr. Carson freely admits the secondary meaning of the word, in the sense of to dye, and even reproves many of his brethren for still denying it.

"Let it here be observed that this secondary meaning of a word is just as *real and literal* as the primary one. Indeed, there are multitudes of instances, in all languages, where it is the only existing meaning. The primary meaning has fallen into disuse, or perhaps is lost. Thus the primary meaning of our English word *prevent* is 'to go before,' and, when our version of the Bible was made, that meaning was in use. Thus David says, (Ps. 119: 107) 'I prevented the dawning of the morning.' (Ps. 88: 13.) 'In the morning shall my prayer prevent thee.' This meaning is now wholly obsolete, and only the secondary one, to *hinder*, to *obstruct*, remains. So the word *pagan* at first meant one who dwelt in a village; *heathen*, a heath-dweller; *villain*, a peasant or farm-laborer; *knave*, a boy; *martyr*, a witness, etc. Dr. Carson himself says, 'Nor are such applications of the word to be accounted for by metaphor. They are as literal as the primary meaning.' p. 46.

"BAPTIZO has also its primary and secondary meanings. And as this is the very word used by our Lord in appointing his ordinance, and as the question before us is as to its precise meaning, it is necessary here to be somewhat careful in our discriminations.

"A very important distinction in this discussion is that between what are called *general* and *specific* words. A general word denotes an act, but does not tell how that act is done; a specific word does both. Thus 'I traveled to Boston,' may mean that I *walked*, or *rode on horseback*, or *rode in the cars*, or *sailed*. The former is a general term; each of the latter a specific one. The latter are often called also *modal* words, because in themselves indicating the mode of the performance.

"Now the question before us is, whether *baptizo* is a modal verb or not. Does it, according to the usage of classic writers, not only command an act, but also specify the *form* of the act, so that the act itself is not done unless it is done in that mode? Baptists with one voice say, yes. 'My position,' says Carson, 'is that it always signifies to dip; *never expressing anything but mode*.' (p. 55.) This, then, will be the first point to test by reference to the classics in the primary use of the word.

" 1. Does baptizo always and invariably signify to *dip?*

" To dip, according to Webster, signifies ' to plunge or immerse; especially to put for a moment into any liquid; to insert in a fluid and withdraw again.' This definition includes three things, viz., to *put in;* to leave in only *a short time;* and to *take out.* The lack of either of these destroys the idea of dipping.

" First, the thing dipped must be *put in.* Whatever is in a fluid, as its natural element, is not dipped. Fishes which swim in the water, and seaweed which grows on the bottom, are not there by dipping. Second, the time of being in must *be short.* A boatman dips his oar, but not his anchor. ' To put *for a moment* into,' says Webster. Third, it must be *taken out.* If it permanently remain, some other term must be used. A ship lost at sea, is not dipped, neither is the Atlantic Cable. These three elements must all enter into the idea of dipping. Thus, we dip a glass of water, we dip our finger in a bowl, we make candles by dipping, etc."

" This shows then," said Mrs. Mason, " that

our baptism is truly and properly a dipping. The person is put into the water for a moment, and is then lifted out. Why is not that the exact thing to be done according to your own showing?"

"It is certainly an exact *dipping*," replied Mr. Stanley, "but for that very reason it is not *baptizing*, in the classic meaning of the Greek word. It corresponds well enough to the word *bapto*, but not to the word *baptizo*. Innumerable instances of the use of the latter word occur, in which one or more of the said elementary ideas are wanting, and some in which they are *all* wanting. Many things in Greek are said to be baptized which are not *put in* at all, many which are not *taken out* at all, and many which remain in *for a long time*."

"You will much oblige me, uncle," said Joseph, "if you will give me some examples confirming these extraordinary statements."

"I will do so, with pleasure. First of baptisms where there is no putting in at all. Aristotle[1] describes a country beyond the Pillars of Her-

---

[1] This and many of the subsequent illustrations are from Dale's "Classic Baptism," one of the ablest and most original works on the mode of baptism ever published.

cules, having shores 'full of rushes and seaweed, which, when it is ebb tide, are not *baptized*, but when it is full tide are flooded.' Diodorus Siculus, describing the annual inundation of the Nile, says, 'Many of the land animals being surrounded, perish, being *baptized*; but some fleeing to higher places are saved.' In neither of these cases is there any dipping at all. The sea coast is not put into the water, but the tide rolls in and overflows it. The animals are not plunged into the Nile, but the water rises over them, till they are suffocated.

" Next of baptisms when there is no *taking out*. The instance last cited is an example. When the Nile baptized the cattle by overflowing them, it neither put them in nor took them out; they were left in the water. Dion Cassius says, 'The vessels which were in the Tiber — were *baptized*,' —*i. e.* sunk. Indeed this is a very common expression applied to vessels that are foundered, and lost beneath the waters. No restoration of them is implied.

" And the same example illustrates the third class of baptisms, where the continuance in that state is not brief. A sunken ship ordinarily remains such. Plutarch speaks of arrows, helmets and pieces of iron breast-plates and swords, relics of an ancient battle, found *baptized* in the marshes. They had been there too long to be call dipped.

"So then the word *baptizo*, even in its primary, literal meaning, does not necessarily imply a single one of the ideas entering into the word dip. It is doubtful whether in the whole range of Greek literature, it ever once expresses the complex act performed by the Baptists in administering the Christian sacrament. That act is properly denoted by *bapto*, not baptizo; and should be called a *bapting* not a baptizing. The New Testament knows nothing either of the name or the thing."

"But Dr. Carson insists," said Joseph, "that baptizo has its modal meaning in the passages you have cited."

"I am aware he does, but with a degree of hardihood which can never be sufficiently admired. The 'modal meaning,' you remember, is to *dip*. 'It always signifies to dip.' Of course, it must here be 'a figure.' No matter what the act spoken of is, it is always a 'figure of dipping.' Washing of table-couches was a dipping, Christ's agony on the cross was a dipping, now the overflowing of the tide is a dipping. I presume it would be impossible to name an act, not even to *sprinkle* itself, (since poor Nebuchadnezzar, he says, was dipped in the night-dews) which, if his theory required it, would not be a dipping. Observe now, this is not argument; it is simple *assertion*, and one that insults the common-sense of his readers. Of course, no reasoning can refute it. The only answer it deserves is to leave it unanswered to the consciences of those who, on such grounds, are invited to excommunicate all undipped persons from their fellowship.

"2. Does baptizo, as its modal meaning, signify to *plunge?* The question is speedily answered. The word plunge, like dip, denotes the act of *putting into*, with the additional idea of force or swiftness. It differs from dip, in that it does not imply *taking out of.* I plunge into a stream; I plunge a sword into an enemy, etc. But the instances cited, show that baptizo does not mean that. The shore was not plunged into the rising tide; the land animals were not plunged into the inundation, etc. Certainly, the modal meaning is not to be found in this word."

"I have observed, father," said Mary, "that

you have not mentioned the word *immerse* in this connection at all. I think Baptists are now most accustomed to use that word, are they not?"

"It is the one," said Arthur, "that they have chosen for translating baptizo in their new version of the Bible."

"Yes," said Mr. S., "but the remarkable thing about it is that this is *no modal word at all*, any more than the word travel! A man may travel in half-a-dozen different ways, and a thing may be immersed in as many. 1. It may be put into water. 2. Water may flow over it, as the incoming tide covers the shore. 3. Water may be poured upon it till it is covered. 4. It may be wrapped about till completely invested. Dr. Kane spoke of himself and his men, as immersed in their fur garments. 5. It may be inclosed without any act whatever, as an oyster growing on a rock under a water is immersed. 6. It may be inclosed by the withdrawal of something else, as, when a light is extinguished, a person is immersed in darkness. Here, then, is a single condition, — that of *being within some enveloping element*, but it is caused in six different modes, and perhaps as many more might be conceived of. Now, which of all these is the *one* modal act of immersion, that which signifies 'mode and nothing else'?"

"But, Mr. Stanley," asked Nellie, "do you mean to say that *baptizo*, in classic usage, is applicable to as many different acts as that? For, if you do, it settles the whole question."

"I do mean to say it may be applied to as many different acts as that, and more, to cause the condition referred to, as witness the following examples.

"1. To *put within*. 'I *baptized* him — *i. e.*, Cupid, — into the wine.' Julian.

"2. To *overflow*. 'Sea coasts which at ebb tide are not *baptized*.' Aristotle. 'Many of the land animals surrounded by the river perish, *being baptized*.' Diodorus Siculus.

"3. To *carry down*, as a swollen river bears away in its current. 'The stream carrying down many, *baptized* them.' Ib.

"4. To *dash over*, as by the crest of a wave. 'I am one of those *baptized* by that great wave'. Libanius.

"5. To *wade in*. 'The army marched all day, *baptized* up to the waist.' Strabo. 'They marched through with difficulty, the infantry being *baptized* up to their breasts.' Polybius.

"6. To *sink by its own weight*. 'They perished, some in embarking upon the boats thrown down by the press, others even in the boats, *baptized* by their own weight.' Dion Cassius. 'They were *baptized* by their full armor.' Suidas.

"7. To *dwell in*, as the soul in the body. 'They have the soul very much *baptized* by the body.' Achilles Tatius. 'They have their nature and perceptive power *baptized* in the depth of the body'. Aphrodisias.

"8. To be in by the *withdrawal* of a surrounding element. 'I saw a vessel *baptized* in a calm.' Char. Aph. In this case, the winds being withdrawn, the vessel was left in a condition of repose.

"Glance now through these examples, and you will see that while they all represent the object as being in an enveloped condition — a state of *inness*, if I may so say — the acts by which this is caused are exceedingly varied. Notice, especially, that in none of them was the act a dipping. In the first instance Love (Cupid) was not put in and taken out again, but left in and drank in the wine. In none of them could the word baptism be translated by dip. In all of them it may be translated by immerse; showing that dip is a modal verb and immerse is not. What is plainer then, than that baptizo instead of being always a modal word, 'signifying nothing but mode,' is *never* one; and so that the very foundation of the Baptist assumption, tested even by the classics themselves, is unsound?"

"But, uncle," said Joseph, "this, surely, is an excess of refinement. You are making distinctions which are of no practical importance. The essential fact remains, in every case you have cited, that baptizo causes its object to *be wholly in or under the element used.* This is enough for us. If this state or condition is attained, the precise mode in which it is done is of no importance."

"What! The *mode* of no importance. Is it possible that I hear a Baptist saying that? Is not this whole dispute about the *mode* of baptism? Have we not been told ten thousand times that *baptizo* is a specific or modal word, that, 'when first applied to this ordinance,' as Carson says, 'it not only contained a specific mode, but it expressed nothing but a specific mode. *Mode was its very essence*'? (p. 243.) And when I ask you, out of the examples I have adduced, to state which of these acts is the modal one, do you tell me it is to immerse, which is not modal at all, and then finally conclude that the mode is of no importance?"

"But you evade the essential thing, viz., *the condition of inness*, as you call it. To be baptized, a person must have been caused to be wholly in or under the water. This is the thing for which we contend, whatever be the act which causes it."

"Well, then, let us look after that," said Mr. S. "Hitherto we have been examining only the primary meaning of the word, in which it is conceded that this condition of *inness* is an essential idea. But when we pass from this to its secondary meanings, even this totally disappears. Objects immersed are for the most part affected by the element surrounding them, and thereby come into a new state or condition. Thus a man placed under water is *distressed* by suffocation; he is *benumbed* by it; he is *stupified;* he is *bewildered;* he is made *unconscious;* he is *drowned.* Often things are more favorably affected; they may be *softened*, and *warmed*, and *exhilarated*, and *vivified*, and *cleansed*. Next, by a process customary in all languages and with almost all words, the force of the word, passing by the immediate and causal act, rests on the *effect* alone, irrespective of the mode in which it is caused. Instead of being stupefied, for example, by submersion under water, it denotes being stupefied in any way, where there is no immersion at all, and where even no fluid of any sort is used, as by swallowing a poisonous drug. In fact, any thing liquid or solid, material or immaterial, which is able *powerfully to affect* a person, is capable of baptizing him in the Greek sense of the word. This will be illustrated by the following examples.

"*Baptism with a drug.* 'Satyrus had somewhat left of the drug by which he had put Conops to sleep. Of this, while serving us, he pours secretly into the last cup which he brought to Panthia. She, rising, went into her chamber and immediately slept. But Leucippe had another servant whom, having *baptized* with the same drug,' etc. *Achilles Tatius.* Here it is said that Satyrus baptized a person with an opiate drug; *i. e.* put him into a state of insensibility. Plainly the intent was to denote the *effect* simply, without describing the physical form of the act. Or if one persists in demanding that form, we find it not in dipping the person into the opiate, but in causing him to swallow it.

"*Baptism by wine.* 'Thebe exhorted to the murder; and having with much wine baptized Alexander and put him to sleep,' etc.,— *Conon.* The *form* of this baptism was pouring the wine into him, not plunging him into it. This was a very common use of the word among the Greeks. 'You seem to be baptized with unmixed'— *i. e.* strong —'wine.' *Athenaeus.* 'Then powerfully baptizing, he set me free.' *Ib.* 'I myself am of these who yesterday were baptized,' *i. e.* intoxicated. *Plato.* 'The nobleman being sober and prepared, set upon us drunken and baptized,' *Plutarch.* 'Of those slightly intoxicated, only the intellect is disturbed, but the body is still able to obey its impulses, being not yet baptized.' *Ib.*

"*Baptism with taxes.* 'On account of the abundant revenue from these sources, they do not baptize the people with taxes.' *Dio. Siculus.* The word denotes the *effect*, viz., to oppress. There is no allusion here to any form of the act by which they are *put into* taxes. The ideas of dipping, plunging, immersing are not only wholly wanting, but they cannot be forced upon the sentence without the utmost incongruity.

"*Baptism with diseases, etc.* 'But when he

does not so continue, being baptized with diseases and the arts of wizards.' *Plotinus.* Here is a man overcome by disease and the magic incantations of sorcery. Is he immersed within them?

"*Baptism with grief.* 'Grief for him baptizing the soul, and darkening the understanding, brings a certain mistiness over the eyes.' *Libanius.* 'Let us not be co-baptized by this grief of his, nor be unobservantly carried away by his tears.' *Heliodorus.*

"*Baptism by misfortunes.* 'Misfortunes falling upon, baptize us.' *Achilles.* The effect is to distress us; the form of the act is to fall upon, as a tempest or shower. If we must make baptizo a modal word, it is here certainly a sprinkling or pouring.

"*Baptism by questions.* 'I, knowing that the youth was baptized, wished to relieve him.' *Plato.* The young man was embarrassed or confused by the sophistical questions put to him.

"*Baptism by excessive labors.* 'As plants are nourished by water in measure, but are choked by excess, after the same manner the soul grows by labors, in measure, but is baptized by excess.' *Plutarch.* How idle is it to inquire for the form of the act here. If we *must*, we shall find it not in the figure of an immersion but of excessive rains that drown the vitality of tender plants.

"*Baptism with sleep.* 'Midnight was baptizing the city with sleep.' *Heliod.* Baptists translate this, 'had plunged the city in sleep,' but this is to violate one of the simplest rules of Greek syntax.

"*Various other baptisms.*

"'What is sudden and unexpected astounds the soul — and baptizes it.'

"'To be baptized with such a multitude of evils.'

"'Since circumstances baptized you.'

"'Having found the unhappy Cimon baptized and forsaken.'

"'Baptized with debts of fifty millions.'

"Such was the mode in which classic Greek authors were accustomed to use this disputed word. The question before us now is, whether they gave to it as to its mother-word, *bapto*, a secondary, as well as primary, signification; that is, one, in which, losing sight of the form of the act, it expressed simply the effect. I do not see how any candid mind, looking at the examples now adduced, can doubt on that point. When a drug baptizes a person, it is not because he is *in* it, overwhelmed by it, or submerged under it. He is not put into it, nor taken out of it; the condition or relation of *inness* is no part of the conception we form of it.

" And if the Greeks, within the carefully regulated limits of their own usage, could thus employ the word to denote *effect* alone, without reference to mode, then might the writers and speakers of the New Testament do the same. They needed to speak of an effect, the greatest, the most momentous, known to man, — the moral renovation of a sinful soul by the Spirit of God. It was not such an effect as the heathen Greeks had ever heard of, or had had occasion to express by any word in their tongue. But they had employed a certain word in a similar way, to denote, in general, *a controlling influence;* and this would amply justify its use, for want of a better, to designate that great spiritual renovation. Therefore, the sacred writers called both it, and the outward rite that symbolized it, a BAPTISM. Nor, in so doing, is there any conceivable reason why the word should be any more confined, or tied down by modal forms, than when used by Plato, or Plutarch, or Heliodorus, to describe the effects of wine, or grief, or oppressive taxes, or any one of the numerous things that exert a controlling influence over men."

"The examples you have now given," said Mary, "are derived wholly, I think from *pagan* Greek authors. Are there none to be adduced from Christians? I don't see why the conversion of a man to Christianity should destroy his ability to speak and write the language with as much purity as before, or as any of the heathen?"

"Very true," said her father. "The custom has been to cite heathen writers only as authorities on this subject. There is no reason, however, why the inquiry should be thus limited. The early Fathers of the church were, for the most part, converts from heathenism, and, of course, had received their language and early training from pagan sources. If their subsequent writings cannot strictly be called classic, in the technical sense of that term, they may still be as good evidence as to the import of these disputed Greek words, as any others of their times. And, for the sake of completeness, I will cite with these some of the early Latin writers."

"Not, however, as specimens of classic *Greek* usage, I trust," said Joseph.

"No; yet certainly, the practice of learned Latin writers in the classic period, cannot be without weight on the subject. The two languages were closely affiliated, and scholars of that age spoke and wrote both, with almost equal ease."

"Well, I do not object to any light which can possibly be derived from this or any other source."

"We have then, first," said Mr. Stanley, "that most able philosopher and scholar of his day, Origen of Alexandria, born A. D. 185. Speaking of Elijah's sacrifice on Mt. Carmel, (1 Kings 18: 32-38), he says, 'Elijah did not baptize the wood of the altar—*ta xyla baptizontos*—but commanded the priests to do it.' Similarly, also, Basil the Great, archbishop of Cæsarea, says, 'Elijah showed the power of baptism upon the altar of burnt offerings, burning the sacrifice not with fire, but with water.' Now, Arthur, will you turn to the passage in Kings, and read it, that we may see what constituted a *baptism* in the estimation of these eminent Greek Fathers?"

Arthur read: "'And he put the wood in order, and cut the bullock in pieces, and laid him on the wood, and said, Fill four barrels, (Heb.

buckets), with water and *pour it* on the burnt sacrifice and on the wood. And he said, Do it the second time, and they did it the second time. And he said, Do it the third time, and they did it the third time. And the water ran round about the altar, and he filled the trench also with water.'"

"Does Dr. Carson explain this application of the word by Origen," asked Mary.

"Oh, yes; he says 'Every child knows that our word immerse may be used in the same way.' And that is all!

"Ambrose, bishop of Milan in the fourth century, a Latin Father, calls the same transaction, a type of baptism;—*typum baptismatis.*

"Cyril, bishop of Jerusalem in the same century, calls the brazen laver of the tabernacle, a 'symbol of baptism,'—*sumbolon tou baptismatos.* This is expressly said to have been made for 'Aaron and his sons to wash their hands and feet thereat.' Ex. 30: 19.

"Clement of Alexandria, one of the most distinguished Greek Fathers, says,—evidently in allusion to Mark 7: 4.—'This is a custom of the Jews, to be baptized often upon a couch—*epi koite baptizesthai.* 'Well, therefore, it is said, Be pure, not by washing, but by thought.'

"Very often do the Fathers, both Greek and Latin, call sprinkling and pouring a baptism. Referring to Ps. 51: 7, Ambrose says, 'He who desired to be cleansed by a typical baptism — *typico baptismate* — was sprinkled — *aspergebatur* — with the blood of a lamb, by a bunch of hyssop.' Again, 'No one can be cleansed from the leprosy of sin by the water of baptism, but under the invocation of the Father, and the Son, and the Holy Ghost.'

"Gregory Nazianzen, Patriarch of Constantinople in the fourth century, exhorts, 'Let us be baptized that we may overcome; let us partake of the purifying waters more powerful than hyssop, more cleansing than the legal blood, more holy than the ashes of the heifer sprinkling the unclean,' etc.

"Jerome, the author of the Latin Vulgate, commenting on Ezek. 36: 25, paraphrases the words of the prophet thus, 'Upon the believing, and those converted from error, I will pour out the clean water of saving baptism.' — *effunderem aquam mundam baptismi salutaris*.

"Didymus of Alexandria, in the fourth century, writes, 'The very image of baptism both continually illuminated and saved Israel at that time, as Paul wrote, (1 Cor. 10: 1), and as Ezekiel prophesied, (36: 25), "I will sprinkle clean water upon you." And David, "Sprinkle me with hyssop."

"Cyril of Jerusalem,—'Thou seest the power of baptism.—Be of good courage, O Jerusalem,—He will sprinkle clean water upon you,' etc.

"Frequently, baptism is employed in the general sense of purification, and without the use of any liquid whatever. Thus, Justin Martyr, born in A. D. 114, calls circumcision itself a baptism. 'What is the message of circumcision to me who have received testimony from God? What need is there of that baptism — *ekeinou tou baptismatos* — to one baptized by the Holy Ghost?' Cyril says, 'Being circumcised, through washing by the Holy Spirit. By the circumcision of Christ, being buried with him by baptism.'

"Ambrose says there are three baptisms, one by water and the Spirit, one, the baptism of Christ's death, and a third by the flaming sword at the gate of paradise. 'There is also a baptism at the entrance of paradise which once did not exist, but after the transgressor was excluded, the flaming sword began to be. Sin began, and baptism began, by which they might be purified who desired to return, that, having returned, they might say, "We have passed over by fire and water."' Ps. 66 : 12.

"This sword, which seems to be affliction or sorrow, Ambrose represents as wielded by Christ himself, in consequence of which, he is named the 'Great Baptizer.' 'Who is it that baptizes by this fire ? He of whom John says, He shall baptize with the Holy Spirit and fire. Therefore, the Great Baptizer will come (for so I name him, as Gabriel did, saying, "He shall be great;" Luke 1: 32), he will see many standing before the entrance to paradise. He will wave the sword turning every way. He will say to those on the right hand, not having weighty sins, "Enter ye who are courageous, who fear not the fire,"' etc. Thus, according to this Father, sorrow is a baptism designed to cleanse from sin, administered by Christ, who is, therefore, called the Great Baptizer, not by dipping, but by waving the sword.

"Origen, in like manner, says, ' The Saviour brings both sword and fire, and baptizes those things which could not be purged by the purification of the Holy Spirit.' We have now nothing to do with the sentiments or reasoning of these

Fathers, but, simply, with their use of the words baptize and baptism.

"In this sense, that suffering was a means of purification, the Fathers were wont to call martyrdom a baptism. Thus Eusebius, the learned Greek historian of the church, who lived in the third century, says, 'Herais, yet a catechumen, received that baptism which is by fire, and departed out of this life.'

"Martyrdom was also called a baptism by blood. Thus Origen, 'That we may leave this world, washed by our own blood. For the baptism of blood only can render us purer than the baptism of water. If God would grant to me that I might be cleansed by my own blood, that I might attain that second baptism, dying for Christ, I would depart out of this world secure.'

"In the same sense, Clement of Alexandria, calls martyrdom a baptism by tears. 'Baptized a second time by tears.'

"In the same line of thought, the sufferings and death of Christ are represented as a baptism that cleanses sinners. So Ambrose: 'There is also another baptism, of which the Lord Jesus says, "I have a baptism to be baptized with, which ye know not." (Luke 12: 10.) And as he had been already baptized in Jordan, this must be the baptism of passion, by which, through his blood, every one of us must be cleansed.' Also Theophylact: 'He calls his death a baptism, as being a purging of us all.' And Tertullian, 'These two baptisms [water and blood] he shed forth from the wound of his pierced side.' And Cyprian, 'The Lord declares in the gospel that those baptized by his blood and passion are sanctified and attain the grace of the divine promise.'

"Confession of sin, as a means of obtaining pardon and moral cleansing, was styled a baptism. Thus Cyprian, in connection with the passage just quoted, refers to the confession of the penitent thief on the cross, as this 'baptism of a public confession and of blood,' which is able to avail for salvation.

"I will cite but two examples more, out of scores that might be given, of the use of baptism by the Fathers, where the idea of immersion is impossible. Origen repeatedly styles the passage of the river Jordan by the Israelites, on their entry into the promised land, a baptism unto Joshua, as the passage of the Red Sea was a baptism unto Moses. 'Paul might say respecting this, " I would not have you ignorant, brethren, that all our fathers passed over through the Jordan, and were all baptized unto Joshua with the Spirit and the river." But Joshua, who succeeded Moses, was a type of Jesus Christ, who succeeded the economy of the law by the preaching of the Gospel. Wherefore, though they all were baptized unto Moses by the cloud and the sea, their baptism had something bitter and unpleasant, because still fearing their enemies.— But the baptism unto Joshua by a truly sweet and potable river has many choice things beyond that.— The Lord said to Joshua, " This day will I begin to magnify thee in the sight of all Israel, that they may know that as I was with Moses, so I will be with thee. Come hither, and hear the word of the Lord our God; by this ye shall know that the living God is among you." For, by the baptism into Joshua, we know that the living God is among us. And the Lord acknowledges the reproach of Egypt to be taken away in the day of the baptism into Joshua, when Joshua thoroughly *purified* the children of Israel.' Now the record of the passage itself will show that there was no possible immersion in this case. Will one of you read it in Josh. 3 : 16, 17 ?

Mary read: "'The waters which came down from above stood and rose up upon a heap very far from the city Adam, that is beside Zaretan, and those that came down toward the sea of the plain, even the Salt Sea, failed, and were cut off; and the people passed over right against Jericho. And the priests that bare the ark of the covenant of the Lord stood firm *on dry ground* in the midst of Jordan, and all the Israelites passed over *on dry ground* until all the people were passed clean over Jordan.'"

"Plainly," said Nellie, "there could have been no immersion here; what then do you think was Origen's idea in this use of the word baptism?"

"Simply that of purification, as his own language intimates. Now only at their actual entrance into Canaan is the promise of God to their fathers fulfilled. The reproach of Egypt — their bondage and pollution in a foreign land — is taken away. The miraculous passage of the river is both their purification and a sacrament of obedience to Joshua as their leader under Jehovah. The baptism was a purely ideal one, in which the mind of the writer rests wholly upon the spiritual significance of the event, and not upon the form.

"The other instance is from the writings of the same author, in which he represents the miraculous dividing of the waters of the Jordan, by the prophet Elijah, and his passing over on dry ground, a baptism. 'Elias, when about to be received up into heaven, having taken his mantle and wrapped it together, smote the water which divided hither and thither; and they both passed through, to wit, he and Elisha; for he is more fitted to be taken up having baptized himself by the Jordan,' etc. Origen's idea in this case seems to have been much the same as in the preceding, that this 'dry baptism' was a special *purification* which fitted the soul of the prophet for heaven.

"On this subject Bingham remarks, 'From the ceremonies used in the act of administration it took the peculiar names of *baptism, tinction,* and *laver* of regeneration, which properly denote either an immersion in water, or such a washing or sprinkling as was used among the Jews in some cases, and among Christians when they had occasion to baptize sick persons upon a deathbed. For then baptism was administered by sprinkling only, and not by dipping or immersion. So that it must be noted that baptism in the ancient style of the church, *does not absolutely and necessarily import dipping or immersion*, though that was the more usual ceremony, practiced heretofore as well upon infants as adult persons,' etc. Antiquities, vol. 1. p. 477.

"I am now ready," said Mr. Stanley, "to submit the question, as cousin Joseph would say, to my jury, even though he himself be one of them, whether or not baptizo has been proved to have a secondary meaning — one or more. In view of these examples from Greek authors, pagan and Christian, of the classic times, what is to be said of the assertions of Dr. Carson that 'baptizo in the whole history of the Greek language has but one meaning. It not only signifies to dip or immerse, *but it never has any other meaning.*' (p. 19). 'It always signifies to dip, never expressing anything but mode,'" p. 55.

"I think," replied Joseph, "it must be conceded that his language is too sweeping. I am happy to add that all our writers are not like him."

"No, certainly not in their rudeness and dogmatism, but as a rule they are equally positive in their statements. There is no man in the denomination, perhaps, of greater ability and learning, than Prof. T. J. Conant of N. York; and his language is this, 'The word baptizo during the whole existence of the Greek as a spoken language had a *perfectly defined, and unvarying import*,' and that, 'nothing more than *the act of immersion*.' And generally the reasoning of Baptists as to the meaning of the word may be summed up in three propositions: —

"1. In many instances baptizo *clearly and plainly* has the sense to immerse.

"2. In other cases it *may* have the sense to immerse. Therefore

"3. In *all* cases it *has* the sense to immerse.

"The main stress of the contest is of course on the second of these propositions. Of Dr. Carson's great work of five hundred closely printed octavo pages, it is safe to say that three fourths are taken up in its support. Here is a large body of examples from Classic, New Testament, and Patristic Greek, where judging from the connection, the scope of the thought, the historical facts involved, and such other things as tend to throw light on the authors' intention, the meaning was in all probability something else than immersion; nay, many, in which the meaning demonstrably could not be immersion. Yet our friends go through all these with a perseverance worthy of a better cause, to prove that, notwithstanding all probabilities, the word *may* have that meaning; or if not, some other, such as to whelm, overwhelm, imbathe, etc., which they quietly assume to be its equivalent. Or if it cannot mean either, literally, they insist that it means it figuratively, finding in the simplest historical statements the most violent metaphors, and when this resource fails, falling back on sheer assertion, and declaring that such *is* the meaning of the word, to be insisted on, as Carson says, even *if it be impossible!* So they come to the third proposition as an inference — Therefore the word in every case has a perfectly defined and unvarying import — nothing more than the act of immersion.

"Then follows the claim that the scholarship of the world is with them; that every one who, on philological or Scriptural grounds, ventures to dissent from this conclusion, shows by that very fact, his ignorance of the subject. You can scarcely take up a Baptist book, or review, or newspaper, wherein these claims are not made and these assertions reiterated.

"Now from all this reasoning and assertion, one

refuge is left us, — *an appeal to the facts.* Here they are, some of them, not all; and the umpire is common sense. We have gone over the Scripture examples first, because most nearly associated with the sacred rite in question, then over the classic and patristic. Remember now that the question is, 'Does baptizo always and only mean to immerse, so that he who is not immersed is not baptized?' and in view of the whole let common sense, enlightened and unbiased, answer."

"There is another topic," said Arthur, "nearly related to this, on which I should be glad to receive some information before we close our conversation for the evening. You have shown us how the Christian fathers used the word baptizo in their writings; and I should like to know what terms were taken as its representative when they translated the Scriptures into other languages. Christ's command to baptize, for instance, — how is it made to read in the *early versions of the New Testament?*"

"I anticipated this inquiry," said his father, "and came prepared to state the facts pertaining to it, so far as they are within my knowledge. It is of no little importance in considering the cotemporary understanding of the meaning of the baptismal words. For it may be assumed that in introducing the Scriptures into a foreign tongue, the utmost care would be taken to make them conformable in every particular to the inspired originals. The words they employed to do this, then, would be the judgment of the translators as to the exact meaning of the corresponding words in the latter.

"Perhaps the earliest version of the New Testament was the Syriac, commonly called the *Peschito* version, a word signifying *pure* or *simple*. An English translation of it by Dr. James Murdock of New Haven, was published a few years ago. 'That version,' says Dr. M., 'was probably made in the very next age after the apostles, by apostolic men, and in a language almost identical with the vernacular tongue of Jesus Christ and his disciples. And it may be supposed that the apostles themselves, and all the first preachers of the gospel among the Syrians adopted this phraseology; and of course that the translators of the Peschito had apostolic authority for their mode of designating baptism.' Am. Bib. Rep. vol. 7, p. 733.

"Now it is very remarkable that in every place

in which baptizo or its derivatives occur in the New Testament, this version employs a word signifying *to stand*. Even John the Baptist is called ' He who causeth to stand.' This is not because the language is destitute of terms signifying to immerse, to pour, to sprinkle, or simply to wash, for it has them all. The explanation, Dr. M. thinks, is that the early Syrian Christians ' associated with the act of baptism the idea of *coming to a stand*, or of taking a public and decisive stand on the side of Christianity. They considered all baptized persons as being established in the Christian faith, and as having made a public profession of that faith, in and by their baptism, so that now they stood before the world as professed or visible Christians.' Accordingly he would read the baptismal commission in Syriac, ' Go ye and teach all nations *making them to stand fast* in the name of the Father,' etc.; also ' He that believeth and *standeth fast* shall be saved,' etc. Dr. M. adds, ' So firmly established and so universally prevalent, among the Syrian Christians, was this custom of denoting baptism by *to stand* and its derivatives, that this usage pervaded all their rituals for public worship, and all the discourses and writings of the Syriac

Fathers. Nor has the usage ever been changed by any Christians using the Syriac language or speaking any modern dialect derived from Syriac. The recent Nestorian version of the New Testament printed at Oroomiah in 1846, every where adopts the usage of the Peschito in the translation of baptizo and its derivatives, except in two instances in which Christian baptism is not intended'—(Mark 7 : 4, and Luke 11 : 38), where the word *wash* is used. 'And the Rev. D. T. Stoddard, one of the missionaries at Oroomiah, who had a hand in bringing out this version, states that among the Nestorian Christians the word *to stand*, is the only term ever used to denote baptism, that they so exclusively appropriate it to this use as never to use it for anything else, and they seem not to know that the word ever had any other meaning.' The Jacobite or *Philoxenian* Syriac version, made probably in the eighth century, closely follows the example of the Peschito.

"The learned historian Augusti, according to Dr. Murdock, accounts for this peculiarity in this venerable version, by the fact that at the time it was made there existed in Syria a sect professing to be disciples of John the Baptist, and calling themselves *Zabians, i. e.* Dippers, from *tseba,* to dip. He supposes the Syrian Christians wished to be distinguished from these, and therefore, for this purpose, and to avoid ambiguity in their theological language, they chose to designate baptism by a word which denotes no outward modal act, but the spiritual import of the rite as they understood it. Ib. p. 743.

"Now all this is significant in the highest degree. Here is the very first version of the New Testament ever made, nearly if not quite in the time of the apostles, in almost the very vernacular of the Lord and of his disciples, — the standard Scriptures of one of the oldest, most venerable, and most numerous branches of the Oriental church, in which the idea of immersion or any other modal act is most carefully excluded from baptism, and from every allusion to it, even in the very name of the Baptist himself. Did the authors of this version, of whom there is a tradition that they were appointed by the apostle Thaddeus himself, (Kitto. Bib. Cyc.) believe that the form was so essential that without it the rite was no baptism? Was the whole Syrian Church, with all its offshoots and descendants, suffered to be built upon an error which would

14

vitiate its very existence and make it no church? Nor was this a possible danger, only, for we shall see hereafter that not only immersion but pouring and sprinkling have been, in fact, practiced in these churches of the far East as valid baptism, and are to this day.

"The oldest *Arabic* version, dating from the seventh century, is believed to have been made from the Syriac, with some alterations, and follows that in the translation of the word baptizo in a majority of places, — Murdock says in forty-nine out of seventy-three, while twenty-four have a word signifying immersion.

"The oldest *Persic* version was also made from the Peschito about the eighth century, It uses a word signifying generally to wash. (Chrystal p. 54.)

"The ancient Egyptian contains three important versions, the *Coptic*, the *Sahidic*, and the *Bashmuric*, all of them dating from the second and third centuries. Two of these transfer the Greek word without translating it; the third is said to use a word signifying to immerse.

"All of the early Latin versions, I believe, without exception, transfer the Greek baptizo, without translating it. This is true of the *Itala*, which Augustine regarded as the best of all, and which goes back, apparently, to the second century, and to usage connected with the apostolic age. (Robinson's Lex. p. 119.) So also with the Latin *Vulgate*, prepared by Jerome, and made the standard authority in the Catholic church, as it has been the mother of nearly all the translations into the various Romanic tongues of modern Europe, our own English included.

"The ancient *Gothic* version, dating in the fourth century, and those of most of the modern languages of the same stock, including the German, Danish, Swedish, Dutch, etc., have the word dip, or its equivalent. The Anglo-Saxon had also the word *fullian*, to cleanse, to bleach, from which comes our word 'fuller.' In Matt. 3: 1, it reads, 'In those days came John the Fuller,' etc. The Icelandic has *skira*, to scour, or cleanse.

"The *Slavonic* dialects, viz., the Russian, Polish, Bohemian, Lithuanian, etc., translate baptizo by a word signifying to *cross*, evidently from the sign of the cross, used in the administration of the rite.

"So far, then, as the early versions are concerned, the weight of their testimony is decidedly against the exclusive claims of immersion. All the oldest and most valuable, with scarce an exception, either translate the word by something different from that, or they transfer it bodily. None of them exhibits such a usage as it should, on the theory of Carson, Conant and others, that it means 'mode and nothing else.' What can more conclusively show that the learned and pious men, who gave these versions to their countrymen, saw no such exclusive meaning in the originals, and felt no obligation to thrust it upon the words which were to teach the will of Christ to mankind?"

"But I have heard it affirmed," said Mary, "that the translators of our English Bible were forbidden by King James to translate baptizo, and were required to transfer it as we now have it."

"Nothing can be more untrue than this. No order to this effect can be found in the instructions given them. Baptize and baptism had been naturalized English words two hundred years, and as such were used by Wiclif himself, in the first English translation ever made, in 1380, in which, as I have said, he followed the example of the Vulgate, and many of the most venerable versions of antiquity. Besides, immersion was not then an English word at all, but Latin."

"But why do you suppose these words were ever transferred, in any language?" asked Arthur.

"Because they are words which, in their religious sense, have a *unique* meaning, which is not conveyed by any uninspired word whatever. Baptizo, in this sense, does not mean to immerse, or sprinkle, or pour, or even, generically, to wash. Even the Baptists, who say it means to immerse, never use it to denote that idea, except when referring to the Christian ordinance. Its force, as the authors of the Peschito understood it, is in its inward spiritual signification. It means to wash with water, in the name of the Trinity, as an emblem of the renewing of the Holy Ghost. What outward act, — what other word, in any language soever, means just that? And, therefore, because there was none, this word, the one which the Holy Spirit himself selected and stamped with his own image, was transferred, like the precious coin struck in the mint of Heaven, which was to pass current in all lands and languages, as the one symbolizing and pledging the grace of our God towards a lost world."

CHAPTER VI.

USAGES OF THE EARLY CHURCH.

"WHAT do you propose to make the topic of consideration this evening?" said Joseph Mason to his uncle at their next meeting.

"Just what will be most agreeable to you, and the rest of our company," responded Mr. Stanley. "There are yet several matters of importance involved in this discussion, and I am ready to take up any of them which may be preferred."

"Suppose, then, we inquire what was the practice of the early church, as to the mode of baptism. We Baptists are accustomed to regard this as strongly favoring our views, and I should have been inclined to urge it with a good deal of confidence, but for the ill success which has so far attended my advocacy of our cause."

"I certainly do not think the testimony of the

early church is so much in their favor as Baptists are in the habit of representing it, but of this we shall be able to judge after we have examined it. Before, however, we proceed to this, let us endeavor to get a distinct idea of the nature of the argument from this source, and the weight that properly belongs to it. Of course, you do not regard the opinions and practice of the early church as *authority*, do you?"

"Oh, no; they are important only as a guide to the right interpretation of the baptismal commission. It is to be presumed that those who lived near the time of the apostles had special advantages for understanding it. They were familiar with the language in which the rite was instituted, and with the mode under which it had been practiced ever since the apostolic days. What, then, they did and said upon the subject, should be taken as a very sure indication of the method originally intended."

"Yes, unless it can be shown that there were influences which caused a departure from the original mode. Neither of us can doubt, for instance, that church government early became a very different thing from what it was in the apostles' day, when the elders ("presbyters") of each church, with one of their number to preside, guided its order and worship. Ambition on the part of the metropolitan ecclesiastics led to usurpations of power which corrupted the simplicity of the primitive pattern, and ultimated in the papacy and the inquisition. So with the sacraments, — before we accept the practice of the early church as a certain guide to their original form, we ought to inquire whether or not there were causes which tended to corrupt the original institution and introduce customs not only unknown to the apostolic practice, but absolutely hostile to it.

"It is well also to remind ourselves that the question before us is as to the *exclusive* claims of immersion. If it could be proved that the early church did in fact practice it, yet nothing would be thereby established as to its *sole* validity. It must be shown that they held with the Baptists that nothing else than immersion was baptism, and that they withheld fellowship from all who had not received it in that method. In other words, the task resting upon these brethren, before they can claim the practice of antiquity in their support, is to prove that the rite was never corrupted, and that it was always as exclusive as to its form as it is with them, — both of which I think we shall see is beyond their power."

"Well, father, we are waiting to hear you in relation to these points," said Mary.

"My first remark then," said Mr. Stanley, "is that as to the practice of the church in the *first* century, there is among the Apostolic fathers, a total *silence*. Those fathers, so called because they were either conversant with the apostles themselves or with their immediate disciples, were Clement of Rome, Ignatius, Polycarp, Barnabas, and Hermas. They often allude to baptism, its signification and its benefits, but there is not a word to show what importance they attached to the mode, or even to show certainly what the mode was. Barnabas once or twice speaks of those who 'go down to the water' — *katabainomen eis to hudor* — a phrase apparently derived from Acts 8: 38, which, as we have seen in the baptism of the eunuch by Philip, determines nothing as to the form. Hermas uses an equivalent Latin expression — *in aquam descendimus*. This language is precisely what would be natural if the rite was performed in the manner which I said was most probable in the case of the eunuch, and which is so constantly exhibited in the pictorial representations of Christ's baptism, which I will presently show you. Neither of these writers speaks of immersion, or uses any word or phrase implying it.

"Now this fact is to my mind very significant. This was the era of planting churches, and introducing the Christian rites into new regions and among people of various languages and races. How often, both among Jews and heathens, must the nature and use of these rites have been explained, and what care taken to guard them from perversions and abuses, such as actually took place among the Corinthians. Yet never do we find in all this period, among all the Christian writers of the apostolic age, any reference at all to the mode of baptism. How can this be accounted for if there was any invariable mode, or if the mode was deemed of any consequence whatever? Our Baptist brethren have now been prosecuting their missionary work about the same length of time. Would it not be easy to find in their missionary literature very many statements as to what they deem the true form of this sacrament? Whence the contrast between these and what we find to be true of the first missionary literature of the church?"

"How was it in the second century?" inquired Arthur.

"Nearly the same as in the first. The Christian writers of this period were Justin Martyr, Irenæus, Athenagoras, Theophilus of Antioch, Clement of Alexandria, Tertullian, and a considerable number of others whose works have mostly perished. Out of all these, two only have left us anything on the subject. The first was Justin Martyr, who was put to death in a persecution in A. D. 168. In his Apology for the Christians, addressed to the Emperor Antoninus Pius, he describes the manner in which converts were then received into the church. He says, 'Then they are conducted by us where there is water, and are regenerated in the same way of regeneration in which we ourselves were regenerated. In the name of God, the Father and Lord of all things, and of Jesus Christ our Saviour, and of the Holy Spirit, they then make the washing in the water, — *loutron poiountai*. For Christ says, "Except ye be born again, ye cannot enter into the kingdom of heaven." And by Isaiah, the prophet, it was said in what way those who have sinned and repented, might escape from their sins. "Wash you, make you clean, etc."' Then after explaining the necessity of the new birth, he adds, 'And this washing — *to loutron*—is called an *enlightening*,' etc.

"Notice now the peculiar language of this Father. In explaining to the Roman Emperor, most carefully, the nature of the initiatory Christian rite, he does not call it immersion nor pouring, nor any other term implying form. He even avoids the word baptism itself, as if feeling that a heathen, with only a heathen's conception of the import of that word, would wholly mistake the Christian idea of it. So he calls it, simply, a *washing*, a term which excludes all idea of form; and '*the* washing,' as if this were the customary designation of the rite. Surely, this is not the way that a Baptist of our day would have spoken of it. The phrase to 'go where there is water,' — *entha hudor esti* — proves nothing. It may suggest that they were accustomed to go out of the church for baptism, to a fountain or a baptistery, as we have evidence that the latter came into use very early, but how, when they reached it, the rite itself was performed, he does not say.[1]

---

[1] In this connection may be cited Justin Martyr's statement that sprinkling with holy water " was invented by demons, in imitation of the true baptism, signified by the prophets, that their votaries, (those

"The other writer of that century who speaks of baptism was Tertullian. He was born about A. D., 140, and wrote a treatise, — ' On Baptism ' — in opposition to a person named Quintilla, who rejected this sacrament altogether. The precise date of it is unknown, but it must have been at the very close of the century, if within it at all. It is in this, that we find the first clear description of the mode of baptism, as then practiced."

"And that was by immersion, was it not?" said Joseph.

"Yes; or rather by triple, or, as they usually called it, *trine* immersion, which ever after, for a thousand years, at least, was the law of the church. Observe now, this was more than a century and a half after the institution of the ordinance, a period as long as from our day back a life time before the Revolution; and during all this period of intense activity, amid all the conquests of the church, and under all its persecutions, no writer, so far as we know, made any allusion to the form of the rite, or so described it,

---

of the demons), might also have their pretended purifications by water." If sprinkling was an *imitation* of the true baptism, then the latter would seem, at least, to include sprinkling. Taylor's Ap. Bap. p. 143.

that we can tell what that form was, while, at the same time, that form, as we are now told, was essential to its reality, so that without it, the rite could not exist, and, of course, the church itself, which could be entered only in that way, be perpetuated."

"Well," said Joseph, "however unaccountable this silence may seem during that period, we have now reached a more certain era. In Tertullian's day the practice undeniably was immersion; and, as you say, it continued such for a very long time thereafter."

"Yes, and the reason unquestionably is, that there had now been fully developed the pernicious doctrine of *baptismal regeneration*. There seems to be an innate tendency in mankind to lose sight of the spiritual, and sink it in what is material. Even in the apostles' day, the Corinthians degraded the sister sacrament of the Supper to the level of a heathen festival. So, too, the Saviour's words to Nicodemus were made to teach the necessity of baptism to salvation, nay, that baptism *is* regeneration. We have seen how Justin Martyr, even, used the term in that sense, as denoting the rite itself. And having reached that point, then the mode of the rite became important. Water having become a saving element — 'aqua salutaris' — the more of it the surer the salvation. Paul's expressions in Rom. 6: 3-6; Col. 2: 12, must be literalized by a *burial* in the water; nay the believer must go down into, and come out of, the water *three times*, as the sun went down and rose again three times while Jesus lay in the grave. Thus IMMERSION AND BAPTISMAL REGENERATION WERE DEVELOPED TOGETHER IN THE EARLY CHURCH. I wish not only to call your attention to the fact, but to give it special emphasis. No trace of the former was found before, or apart from, the latter.

"In the light of these facts we are now prepared to study the testimony of Tertullian and his contemporaries. 'When,' said he, 'we are about to go to the water, we do in the church declare, under the hand of the priest, that we renounce the devil, his pomp, and his angels; then are we immersed three times — *ter mergitamur* — answering somewhat more than the Lord in the gospel prescribed,' *i. e.*, probably in response to inquiries, declaring their faith in respect to other things besides those which were fundamental, as to the person and death of

Christ. In the third century, Hippolytus writes, 'He who goes down with faith into the bath of regeneration is arrayed against the evil one, and on the side of Christ; he denies the enemy, and confesses Christ to be God; he puts off bondage, and puts on sonship; he comes up from baptism, bright as the sun, flashing forth the rays of righteousness; but, greatest of all, he comes up a son of God, and a fellow heir with Christ.' Cyril of Jerusalem is still more explicit. 'After these things, ye were led to the holy pool of divine baptism, as Christ was carried from the cross to the sepulcher, which is before our eyes. And each of you was asked whether he believed in the name of the Father, and of the Son, and of the Holy Ghost, and ye made that saving confession, and descended three times into the water, and ascended again, here also covertly pointing, by a figure, to the three days' burial of Christ. For, as our Saviour passed three days and three nights in the heart of the earth, so you also, in your first ascent out of the water, represented the first day of Christ in the earth, and by your descent, the night; for as he who is in the night sees no more, but he who is in the day remains in the light, so in descending, ye saw nothing as in the night, but in ascending again ye were as in the day. And at the selfsame moment ye died and were born, and that water of salvation was at once your grave and your mother.' Basil of Cæsarea says, — 'In three immersions, and in the same number of invocations, the great mystery of baptism is finished, so that both the figure of death is exhibited, and the souls of the baptized are illuminated by the transmission of the knowledge of God.' Jerome gives a somewhat different view of the import of the triple immersion. 'We are thrice immersed, that the mystery of the Trinity may appear to be but one. It may be called one baptism, because, though we are thrice immersed, on account of the mystery of the Trinity, yet it is reputed one baptism.' After the rise of the Arian controversy, and the prevalent denial of the doctrine of the Trinity, this special significance of the mode of baptism by a triple immersion became the predominant view of Christian writers. That this was the regular mode of baptism is testified by all the Fathers for many centuries."

"I am glad to hear such an admission from a Pedobaptist," said Joseph, with a smile. "It fully confirms our position, that the early churches all practiced immersion."

"The facts of history, I should hope, would not be denied by any body, however they may bear on his personal opinions," said Mr. Stanley. "Let me, however, advise you not to boast too soon of the support of early usage, for it may be found to prove altogether too much for your convenience."

"Did not the Fathers insist that a threefold immersion was *necessary?*" asked Mary.

"Certainly; and their reasoning was almost identical with that of the Baptists in behalf of a single immersion, and, for aught I can see, was just as conclusive. They claimed that it was required by the very terms of the baptismal commission. First, by the word *baptizo*. Prof. Stuart, after citing examples from Tertullian and Jerome, remarks, 'It would appear, then, that a feeling existed among some of the Latin Fathers, when they rendered *baptizo* by *mergito*, that baptizo is, in its appropriate sense, what the grammarians and lexicographers call a frequentative verb, *i. e.*, one which denotes repetition of the action which it indicates. Nor are they alone in this. Some of the best Greek scholars of the present and past age have expressed the same opinion in a more definite shape.' Prof. S., on the whole, dissents from this conclusion, as he does from the similar claim that the word always signifies immersion; nevertheless, the statement is interesting as showing how these Fathers reasoned on the subject. Others argued from the structure of the commission, that the word baptize was to be understood as repeated before each name. Thus Tertullian, — 'Commanding that they should immerse into the Father, and the Son, and the Holy Ghost; not into one, for neither are we immersed once, but three times, at each name into each person.' Chrysostom, — 'Christ delivered to his disciples one baptism in three immersions of the body, when he said to them, "Go teach all nations,"' etc. Jerome did not insist that the triple form was enjoined in the Scriptures, but that it had come down from the apostles by tradition, and was regarded as of equal authority in all the church."

"And I suppose," said Mary, "we may add, as Baptists are wont to do, 'These Fathers understood the Greek, and must have known what the apostles' practice was better than we.' But if they were right, then the latter are as wrong as we are. If three immersions were required, then the rite is not performed if there is but one."

"That is precisely what was then said," replied her father. "The custom of *single* immersion was of heretical origin, growing out of an attempt to evade the argument in behalf of the Trinity, derived from the triple form. The first person who taught and practiced it was Eunomius, an Arian bishop of Cyzicum, A. D. 360. Of the estimation in which he and his heretical innovation was held, Theodoret, bishop of Cyrus A. D. 420, thus speaks, ' He subverted the law of holy baptism, which had been handed down from the beginning from the Lord and the apostles, and made a contrary law, asserting that it is not necessary to immerse the candidate for baptism thrice, nor to mention the names of the Trinity, but to immerse once only into the death of Christ.' In like manner, Sozomen, the learned church historian of the same century wrote, ' Some say that he [Eunomius] was the first who dared to bring forward the notion, that the divine baptism ought to be administered by a single immersion; and to corrupt the tradition which has been handed down from apostles, and which is still observed by all,' — *en pasi*. He calls these

'heretical opinions,' and argues against them in a manner curiously applicable to those who now practice the same. These innovators, he says, regard all who have not been baptized in their way, (*i. e.*, by a single immersion into the death of Christ), as unbaptized persons, and always rebaptize in this way all who join their sect, though they had already been baptized in the usual way, (*i. e.* by three immersions into the Trinity). But, as it is plain that none can perform the rite but those who have themselves received it, so they, having only had the aforesaid three immersions, are, by their own principles, unbaptized. Therefore, both they and their disciples are destitute of the benefits of this saving ordinance, and in danger of dying unbaptized. These statements of Theodoret and Sozomen, in condemnation of single immersion, were confirmed by the highest authority of the age. The 'Apostolic Canons,' falsely ascribed to Clement of Rome, and yet, as Murdock remarks, 'valuable documents respecting the order and discipline of the church, about the third century' decreed:—
'If any bishop or presbyter do not perform three immersions of one initiation, but one immersion, which is given into the death of Christ, let him

be deposed; for the Lord' did not say, " Baptize into my death," but, " Go ye and make disciples of all nations," etc.' Upon this canon, the annotator, Balsamon, (12th century) remarks, ' The canon says, he shall be deposed, as one who acts contrary to the doctrine of the Lord, and who is openly impious.' And Zonaras, (same century), ' To immerse once only the person to be baptized in the holy laver, and to celebrate one immersion only into the death of the Lord, is impious; and the one who so baptizes shall be deposed.'

"This decree was re-affirmed by the second general council held at Constantinople, in A. D. 381. After specifying various classes of 'heretics' who were to be received to the church without rebaptizing upon a written renunciation of their errors, it adds, ' But the Eunomians *who baptize with one immersion* . . . if they wish to be joined to the orthodox faith, we receive as heathens, and on the first day, we make them Christians, on the second, catechumens; then, on the third, we exorcise them with blowing three times in their faces and ears; and then we instruct them, and oblige them to remain some time in the church and hear the Scriptures; and then we *baptize* them.'

"This decree, from a body of so high authority, sufficed to put a stop to the obnoxious practice among the orthodox churches, and we hear nothing more of the single immersion till about the end of the 6th century. Then the matter came up again and in a curious way. 'The Arians in Spain,' says Bingham, ' not being of the sect of the Eunomians, continued for many years to baptize with three immersions; but then they abused this ceremony to a very perverse end, to patronize their error about the Son and Holy Ghost's being of a different nature or essence from the Father; for they made the three immersions to denote a difference or degrees of divinity in the three Divine Persons. To oppose whose wicked doctrine, and that they might not seem to symbolize with them in any practice that might give encouragement to it, some Catholics, [or orthodox] began to leave off the trine immersion as savoring of Arianism, and took up the single immersion in opposition to them.' (Antiq. vol. 1: p. 541.) This practice, however, led to a controversy in the Spanish Church, which was referred to Gregory the Great, bishop of Rome, (A. D. 590) who decided in favor of the single immersion, on the sole ground that he would not countenance the practice of those heretics; and this view was confirmed by a provincial synod at Toledo, in 633. This custom, however, always continued local and exceptional, the great body of the church, west and east, adhering for many centuries later, as the latter does to this day, to the ancient method of trine immersion. But even where tolerated, the single immersion was recognized as a *departure* from the original and normal method, to be defended only on the ground of expediency."

"Do you mean then to say," asked Miss Ashton, "that baptism as it is now practiced by the Baptists, by a single immersion, had no support in the sentiments and usages of the early church."

"I do mean precisely that. It originated among the bitterest enemies of the orthodox faith, the most radical rejecters of the doctrine of the Trinity. It was at once declared to be an innovation and a heresy, contrary to the original institution of Christ, and to the authority of the apostles received by tradition; and whatever presbyter or bishop practiced it was ordered by the highest authority of Christendom, an Ecumenical Council, to be deposed. They who had been baptized in that way were pronounced unbaptized, and could not be received into the orthodox communion without rebaptism in the name of the Trinity. And when, at length, after nearly six hundred years, it gained a footing of toleration, it was confessedly as an innovation, made without any authority except expediency, for the purpose of avoiding symbolizing with heretics, though it was by a branch of the same heretics that the single immersion itself was originated. If there was any custom whatever, which beyond all others was rejected and reprobated by the unanimous voice of the orthodox church for six hundred years, it was this very one of baptism by one immersion, which is now urged upon us as the one having the consent of all antiquity, and absolutely essential to the validity of the rite itself!"

"But the ground of dissatisfaction with it, if I understand you," said Joseph, "was not that it was *immersion*, but that it was a single administration, representing a heresy in doctrine."

"True, and this was a more heinous fault, in the estimation of the church, than pouring or sprinkling would have been. These, as we shall presently see, were in many cases expressly allowed, and were always admitted to be valid;

the other, never. But leaving this matter for the present, let me advert to another practice of nearly equal antiquity and universality in the church, — that of requiring all persons, whether men, women, or children, to receive baptism *wholly divested of their clothing.*

"No custom of antiquity is better established by testimony than this. Thus Chrysostom (Hom. 6.) says, 'Men were as naked as Adam in paradise, but with this difference: Adam was naked, because he had sinned, but in baptism a man was naked that he might be freed from sin.' Ambrose (Ser. 10.) says, 'Naked were we born into the world; naked came we to the baptismal font. . . . How absurd, then, that he whom his mother brought forth naked, and the church received naked, should enter heaven with riches!' Cyril of Jerusalem also testifies, (Cat. Mys. 2), 'As soon as ye came to the baptistery, ye put off your clothes, . . . and being thus divested, ye stood naked, imitating Christ, who was naked upon the cross. . . . Oh wonderful thing! ye were naked in the sight of men, and were not ashamed, in this truly imitating the first man, Adam, who was naked in paradise, and was not ashamed.' Once more: Chrysostom, in describing the violent proceedings of his enemies against him, says, 'They came into the church armed, and by violence expelled the clergy, killing many in the baptistery; by which the women who were at that time unclothed in order to be baptized, were put into such a fright that they fled away naked, and could not stay, in their terror, to put on such clothes, as the modesty of the sex required.' Bingham Antiq. vol. 1: p. 536.

"The universality of this custom is admitted by the Baptist historian, Robinson. 'There is,' says he, 'no historical fact better authenticated than this.' The learned Dr. Wall (Hist. Inf. Bap. Part 2.) says, 'The ancient Christians, when they were baptized by immersion, were all baptized naked, whether they were men, women, or children. The proofs of this I shall omit, because it is a clear case. They thought it better represented the putting off of the old man, and also the nakedness of Christ on the cross. Moreover, as baptism is a washing, they judged it should be a washing of the body, not of the clothes.' He also says, 'They took great care to preserve the modesty of any woman that was to be baptized. There were none but women came near, or in sight, till she was undressed, and her body in the water, then the priest came, and putting her head under the water used the form of baptism. Then he departed, and the women took her out of the water, and clothed her again with white garments.'

"This service in connection with the baptism of females was specially assigned to the deaconesses of the church. Epiphanius, the learned historian of the fourth century, even says they were instituted for the purpose of preserving a due regard for the modesty of the sex.[1]

"This subject, I am aware, is too revolting to dwell upon, yet it is due to the facts of history that it should at least be referred to. If all the facts connected with it could be stated, it would afford one of the most astonishing instances of the extent to which an undue regard for forms and rites might carry even the church. Says the venerable Dr. Miller, of Princeton, 'We have the very same evidence in favor of immersing divested of all clothing, that we have for im-

---

"[1]Est quidem ordo diaconissarum in Ecclesia; sed non est institutus ad functionem sacerdotii, vel ad aliquam ejusmodi administrationem, sed ut muliebris sexus honestati consulatur, sive ut tempore adsit baptismi, sive quando nudandum est mulieris corpus, ne ab iis conspiciatur, qui sacris operantur, sed a sola videatur diaconissa, quæ jussu sacerdotis, curam mulieris gerit dum vestibus exuitur." Taylor's Ap. Baptism p. 168.

mersing at all; that so far as the history of the church subsequent to the apostolic age informs us, these two practices must stand or fall together, and that an appendage to baptism so revolting, so immoral, and so entirely inadmissible, plainly shows that those who practiced it must have been chargeable with a superstitious and extravagant adoption of a mere form, which, from its character, we are compelled to believe was a human invention, and took its rise in the rudeness of growing superstition, perhaps from a source still more impure and criminal.' Inf. Bap. p. 83."

"How long did this extraordinary practice continue?" asked Arthur.

"To a greater or less extent until the time of the Reformation; indeed, in some branches of the church, it survives to the present day. The distinguished Catholic historian Brenner, says, 'For sixteen hundred years was the person to be baptized, either by immersion or affusion, entirely divested of his garments.' Am. Bib. Rep. vol. 3: p. 361."

"Were not other superstitious ceremonies practiced in connection with the administration of baptism?" inquired Mary.

"Oh yes, many. Once having departed from the primitive simplicity of the rite, other steps followed in rapid succession until the institution was scarcely recognizable. Inasmuch as water was endowed with such mysterious efficacy, it was soon thought necessary that it should be consecrated. 'The water,' says Tertullian (De Bap.) 'must first be cleansed and sanctified by the priest, in order that, by its own baptism, it may be able to wash away the sins of the man who is baptized.' Indeed it was supposed to undergo a sort of transubstantiation, like that which was alleged to take place in the bread and wine of the eucharist. It became the blood of Christ, in which believers were washed from every stain. (Bingham, Ant. vol. 1: p. 534.)

"Anointing with oil soon followed; then exorcism, or driving away the devil; then the laying on of hands, in token of the reception of the Holy Ghost. Insufflation, or breathing upon the candidate, was another ceremony of like import. Then persons had their eyes anointed with clay, in imitation of the healing of the blind man, (John 9: 6), and their ears opened with the word Ephphatha, (Mark 7: 34). Inasmuch as the baptized were newly born, honey and milk were administered to them, as suitable food for babes; a pinch of salt, symbolical of wisdom, was laid upon their tongues; the head was solemnly covered and uncovered, to denote the attainment of spiritual freedom; the sign of the cross applied; followed by the kiss of peace, and sometimes by the washing of the feet. Lastly, they were clothed in white garments as an emblem of innocence, which they were to wear for eight days, and provided with lighted torches, 'as a figure of those lamps of faith wherewith bright and virgin souls shall go forth to meet the Bridegroom.'" Coleman Anc. Christ. pp. 367-373.

"You spoke just now," said Arthur, "of the baptism of children as well as of men and women. Do you then regard it as certain that the early church practiced infant baptism?"

"As certain as that they baptized at all. Allusions to it are found in the writings of the very earliest Fathers. Thus Hermas, in the apostolic age, says, 'The seal of the Son of God is necessary for every one to enter into the kingdom of heaven,' and 'that seal is baptism.' He held, of course, that infants are saved, pronouncing them 'valued by our Lord and esteemed first of all.' Justin Martyr (born A. D. 114) says, 'I know many of both sexes, sixty and seventy years old, who were made disciples to Christ from childhood.' Irenæus, the disciple of Polycarp, born before the death of the apostle John, speaks of infants and little ones — *infantes et parvulos* — who were 'regenerated unto God' — the customary term, in that age, denoting baptism. Tertullian, who is often quoted by the rejecters of pedobaptism as one who opposed it, nevertheless bears witness to its prevalence in his day, and gives his advice, not against the practice itself, but in favor of some delay in its administration. Origen (born A. D. 185) says, expressly, 'The church had from the apostles the tradition to give baptism to young children'; also, 'according to the usage of the church, it is likewise given to little children.' From that time onward, infant baptism is habitually spoken of as a universal practice. Augustine (born A. D. 354) declares it to be 'that which the universal church holds, and not instituted by councils, but was ever in use, and most rightly believed to be handed down by none other than apostolical authority.' I need not, however, go into the matter at length, for it is a subject foreign to our present purpose."

"We freely concede," said Joseph, "that infant baptism was early introduced into the church, and we account for it, as you do for immersion, in the prevalence of the unscriptural doctrine of baptismal regeneration. But this does not prove that it was practiced by Christ or the apostles."

"And yet you argue from the early prevalence of immersion that *that* was practiced by them. You are strangely inconsistent in your reasoning, for if the argument is good for anything in the latter case, it is in the former. But without stopping now to determine whether infant baptism *originated* in the doctrine of baptismal regeneration or not, there can be no doubt that that doctrine would, at least, tend to the conservation of that rite, and give it universal acceptance. The doctrine, as we have seen, appears in the very earliest uninspired writings in the apostolic age, and is so far a corroboration of the statements of Origen and Augustine, that the rite itself was derived from the apostles."

"I have often," remarked Mary, "heard it said by Baptists that infant baptism is a relic of popery, but according to the evidence now given, it was the universal custom of the church centuries before the papacy began."

"Yes. It is one of the unhappy instances where use is made of prejudice rather than of argument or fact, to excite odium against a matter in controversy. It is devoutly to be hoped that the time is not distant when good men will not feel their need of defending their positions by *such* methods."

"We have now," continued Mr. Stanley, "seen what was the *regular* way of administering baptism in the churches of the third and following centuries. It was by a *triple immersion* of either *adults or infants*, in *a state of nudity*, accompanied by a variety of superstitious ceremonies emblematic of *regeneration*, which was believed to be effected in this sacrament. But this historical survey would be extremely defective if I did not add that there was also a very different mode which, in certain specified circumstances, was allowed, and even in all cases was held to be valid, viz., the method of SPRINKLING OR POURING."

"Will you be good enough to state the proof of that fact?" said Joseph.

"I was about to do so," replied Mr. Stanley. "When the early churches had developed this 'regular' mode of baptism, and, by the authority of bishops and councils, established it as the law of the ordinance, they found that they had imposed on themselves a rite which, for large numbers of persons, was too heavy to be borne. The sick, the infirm, tender infants, individuals at the point of death, etc., could not receive it. And yet the reception of it was believed to be indispensable to salvation. The words of Christ to Nicodemus, 'Except a man,' they read, and rightly too, ' Except a person,' *i. e. any* person — *ei me tis* — ' be born of water and of the Spirit, he cannot enter into the kingdom of God.' Here then, they were in great straits. If this was the sole way of salvation, it was to multitudes a hard way. Christ's yoke was not easy, nor his burden light.

"What should be done in such cases? They could not give up their sick and dying friends to assured perdition; and they could not hasten their death by carrying them to a river or pool, to be stripped naked and plunged thrice beneath the waters. In this emergency, affection and common sense triumphed over ritualism and superstition. They forgot the 'modal' meaning of baptizo; they forgot the necessity of a literal 'burial with Christ' in the baptismal waters, and concluded that it was sufficient, after all, to baptize by sprinkling or pouring of the water, in the name of the Trinity.

"The first formal deliverance on this subject was that of Cyprian, bishop of Carthage, and sixty-six other bishops then attending a council in that city, A. D. 255. The growing tendency to magnify forms had awakened doubts whether these simpler modes of baptism were valid, and a country clergyman, named Magnus, addressed a letter to the bishop, asking his opinion. Cyprian's reply was as follows: — ' You have asked me, my dear son, my opinion concerning those who have obtained the grace of God in infirmity and weakness, whether they are to be regarded as lawful Christians since they have not been washed, but affused with the saving water. In this matter, our diffidence and modesty prejudge no one, that he should not believe as he thinks, and act as he believes. As our humble opinion conceives, we think that the divine benefits can not be curtailed or weakened, nor that anything which is derived from the divine gifts can be diminished, when it is received with a full and entire faith on the part of both the administrator and the receiver. For in the saving sacrament, the defilements of sins are not washed away, like the impurity of the skin and the body, in a carnal and secular bath, so that there is need of soap and other helps, and of a tub or pool, by which the body can be washed and cleansed. In another way the breast of the believer is washed; in another way the mind of man is cleansed, through the merits of faith. In the saving sacraments, when necessity requires, and God bestows his own indulgence, *Divine compends,*' *i. e.,* abridgements of form, 'confer the whole benefit upon believers.[1] Nor ought it to trouble any one that the sick are sprinkled or poured upon, since they attain the grace of the Lord, for the Holy Scripture says, by the prophet Ezekiel, (ch. 36: 28) "Then will I sprinkle clean water upon you," etc. And again, (Numb. 19: 13, 20), "That soul shall be cut off because the water of separation was not sprinkled upon him; he shall be unclean." And again, (Numb. 8: 7), "Sprinkle water of purifying upon them." And again, (Numb. 19: 9), "The water of separation is a purification from sin." HENCE IT APPEARS THAT SPRINKLING OF WATER ALSO

---

[1] In sacramentis salutaribus, necessitate cogente. et Deo indulgentiam suam largiente, totum credentibus conferunt divina compendia.

HATH LIKE FORCE WITH THE SAVING BATH; and when these things are done in the church, where there is a sound faith both of the receiver and the administrator, ALL IS VALID, and may be consummated and perfected by the authority of the Lord, and the truth of faith.'[1]

"Observe here, that Cyprian and his council do not put this shorter mode upon any ground of *human* authority, as if it was an attempt to dispense with a positive law of Christ. On the contrary, he expressly speaks of it as taking place under divine sanction. It is because 'God bestows *his own indulgence*'; the briefer ceremonies are '*divine compends*.' Certainly, this is all that was or could have been claimed for the fuller form. In a word, both were, in his view, clothed with the same authority, and were equally valid.

"The baptism of the sick in such circumstances was called clinic baptism, from *kline*, a couch. Eusebius mentions a person named Novatian, who, being sick and near to death, as was supposed, was baptized on his bed by affusion,

---

[1] Unde apparet aspersionem quoque aquæ instar salutaris lavacri obtinere, et quando hæc in ecclesia fiunt, ubi sit et accipientis et dantis fides integra, stare omnia, et consummari ac perfici posse majestate Domini et fidei veritate.

but afterwards recovered and was ordained to the ministry."

"But you are aware, uncle," said Joseph, "that the Fathers did not call this a proper baptism, but only a substitute for baptism. In this case of Novatian, it was called *perichism*, from *peri*, around, and *cheo*, to pour, because the water was poured around him in his bed."

"But listen again to Cyprian," said Mr. Stanley, "and see whether he regarded this as only a substitute for baptism. 'Some say of those who have attained the grace of Christ by the saving water and lawful faith, that they are not *Christians* but *clinics*.' Such persons he reproves, saying, 'If any one supposes they have received nothing, because they have only been poured upon — *perfusi* — with the saving water, and are destitute and empty still, let them not be so mistaken as to be rebaptized should they recover from their illness and get well. If they must not be rebaptized who have once been consecrated by canonical baptism, why should they be made to distrust their own faith and the favor of the Lord? If they have attained divine grace, so as to be acknowledged as Christians, though by a shorter and smaller measure of the divine gift and of the Holy Spirit, are they not, nevertheless, to be esteemed equal to others?'

"This decision of Cyprian and his associates was accepted by the whole church, and became the recognized practice for many ages. Theologians, historians, councils, and liturgies, refer to it and sanction it. 'The references to baptism of the sick,' says Chrystal,[1] 'are quite frequent after his time. Such baptism the church viewed as valid, without, so far as I have been able to discover, a single dissentient voice, until the seventeenth century.'" p. 171.

"But it was permitted only in cases of *necessity*, I think you observed," said Joseph.

"Yes; it was not the regular mode for others, and yet, in all cases, it was admitted to be valid."

"What was the distinction," asked Nellie, "between regularity and validity?"

"To be *regular* was to be in *the prescribed form*, according to the decrees of the church; to be *valid* was to have the *essence of the rite*, that which made it a *real* though informal baptism,

---

[1] "History of the Modes of Christian Baptism, by Rev. James Chrystal," a very valuable work on that subject.

or, in accordance with the views of those times, to be actually effective to salvation."

"Do the Baptists, Cousin Joseph, at the present day, practice clinic baptism?" asked Arthur.

"I think not. I have never heard that they do so, in any circumstances."

"Joseph is right," said Mr. Stanley. "I have it from a friend, an excellent Baptist minister, who says, 'In no case whatever, does our denomination practice clinic baptism. I know of no instance of the kind in this country or abroad. Baptism with us is not a saving ordinance, and if a proper subject for baptism as to his faith *cannot* receive the ordinance on account of physical disability, he does well as to his purpose in heart therefor, and is accepted of God.'"

"Both in theory and practice then," said Mary, "the early — nay, the universal church, differed totally from the modern Baptists. These do not baptize the sick, nor admit that sprinkling or pouring *is* baptism at all, under any circumstances."

"No; and besides, the ancient church did not rebaptize any who had received 'the compends,' as Cyprian called them; the Baptists, we know, uniformly do. This is another particular in which their practice is condemned by the unanimous voice of Christendom, ancient and modern, their own denomination excepted."

"Was there any thing besides sickness, which was allowed as being within the rule of necessity?" asked Nellie.

"Oh yes; many things. Indeed, the rule was in some instances, interpreted in a very liberal way. Among these were, 1. The *absence of a sufficient supply of water.* The historian Nicephorus, in the 'Magdeburg Centuries,' relates that a Jew, in the second century, traveling through a desert in company with some Christians, was converted, and being taken sick requested baptism. Having no water, they sprinkled — *conspersere* — him with sand, in the name of the Trinity. He unexpectedly recovered and was taken to Alexandria, where his case was laid before the Greek bishop, who decided that the baptism was valid, provided only that he should anew be perfused or sprinkled with water. Miller, p. 81. — 2. *Confinement in prison.* Five martyrs of Samosata are mentioned, who sent from the prison, where they were awaiting execution, for a presbyter to bring a vessel of water and baptize them.[1] In the third century, Laurentius,

---

[1] Fairchild on Baptism. p. 106.

a Roman deacon, was brought to the stake to suffer martyrdom, when one of the soldiers was so impressed that he professed to be converted, and desired to be baptized on the spot. For this purpose, a pitcher of water was brought—*urceo allato*—and the soldier was baptized by the martyr at the place of execution.[1]— 3. When the candidate was *too large*, or the baptistery *too small.* 'It ought to be noted' says Strabo, (sixth century), 'that many have been baptized not only by immersion but by pouring, and so it can still be performed if there be necessity, as we read in the passion of St. Laurentius, that one was baptized from a pitcher which had been brought in. This even *usually happens* when the large size of the bodies of the more mature, and the small size of the vessel which serves as a font, renders it impossible that they should be immersed.' De. Reb. Eccl. 26. So, too, Duns Scotus, the metaphysical theologian of the 13th century, says, 'A minister may be excused from trine immersion; for example, in case he should be feeble as to strength, and there should be a *huge country fellow*— *et sit unus magnus rusticus* —to be baptized, whom he could neither plunge in nor lift out.' Am. Bib. Rep. 3. p. 379.

---

[1] Wall's Hist. See also p. 259.

"These instances are sufficient to show the principles which guided the usage of the times. The triple, nude immersion was regular, and by custom and canon law required in ordinary cases; but when impracticable, dangerous, or inconvenient, the 'compends' were permitted, and their validity as true baptism fully recognized."

"You have spoken," said Joseph, "of the ancient baptisteries used in the church. Some of these, you are aware, are preserved to this day, and show for themselves that they were of sufficient size to allow of the immersion of the largest person."

"*Fonts*, you mean, I suppose. The baptistery was properly the edifice, usually adjacent to a church, in which the font stood; the font was the vessel or receptacle containing the water in which the baptism took place. Many fonts were large enough to admit of the immersion of an adult, and on the other hand, many were so small that they would suffice only for that of infants, — some even not for that.

"The best authenticated representations of the ancient modes of baptism are to be found in the Catacombs of Rome. In these vast cemeteries, dating back to the beginning of the Christian era, where rest the noble army of martyrs, confessors, and saints, who were entombed here during the first four centuries — the period of the Pagan persecutions — are found innumerable illustrations of the social and religious life of the primitive Christians. From the full and admirable work of Withrow[1] recently published, I extract the following statements in relation to this subject: —

"'The testimony of the Catacombs respecting the mode of baptism, as far as it extends, is strongly in favor of aspersion or affusion. All their pictured representations of the rite indicate this mode, for which alone the early fonts seem adapted; nor is there any early art evidence of baptismal immersion. It seems incredible, if the latter were the original and exclusive mode, of apostolic and even Divine authority, that it should have left no trace in the earliest and most unconscious art-record, and have been supplanted therein by a new, unscriptural, and unhistoric method. It is apparent, indeed, from the writings of the fourth and fifth century, that many corrupt and unwarranted usages were introduced

---

[1] "The Catacombs of Rome, and their Testimony relative to Primitive Christianity. By Rev. W. H. Withrow, A. M."

in connection with this Christian ordinance, that greatly marred its beauty and simplicity. It is unquestionable that, at that time, baptism by immersion was practiced with many superstitious and unseemly rites... But in the evidences of the catacombs, which are the testimony of an earlier and purer period, there is no indication of this mode of baptism, nor of these dramatic accompaniments. The marble font represented in the accompanying engraving, now in the crypts

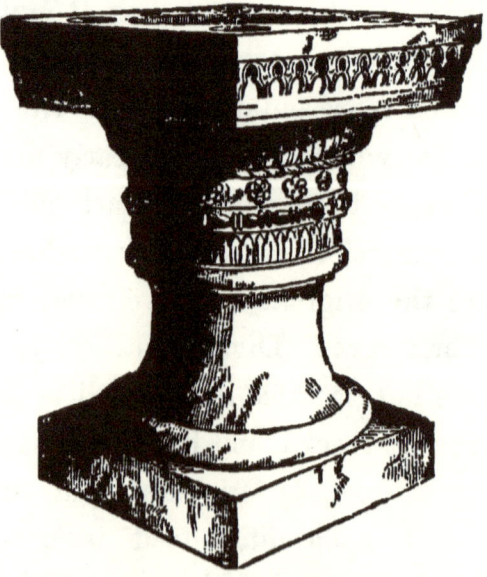

of St. Prisca, within the walls, is said to have come from the catacombs and to have been used for baptismal purposes by St. Peter himself; in

The Baptism of Christ, as shown in the Catacomb of Pontianus.
Page 255.

corroboration of which legend, it bears the somewhat apocryphal inscription $\overline{\text{SCI}}$. PET. BAPTISMV. The tradition at least attests its extreme antiquity, and its basin is too small for even infant immersion.

"' Other fonts have been found in several of the subterranean chapels, among which is one in the Catacomb of Pontianus, hewn out of the solid tufa, and fed by a living stream. It is thirty-six inches long, thirty-two inches wide, and forty inches deep, but is seldom near full of water. It is obviously too small for immersion, and was evidently designed for administering the rite as shown in the fresco which accompanies it.' (pp. 535-537.)

"This fresco is upon the wall directly over the head of the font. It represents our Lord standing naked in the water, while John in his camel's hair raiment is upon the bank, with his right hand placed upon the Saviour's head, as if applying the water thereto. The Holy Spirit descends in the form of a dove; an angel stands by as a witness of the rite; and in the foreground a stag, the emblem of a fervent Christian, is drinking at the stream. The aureola around the heads of these figures indicates, according to

Withrow, a date later than that of the font itself; but that it is very ancient cannot be doubted. See the engraving opposite.

"'In a very ancient crypt of St. Lucina is a another partially defaced baptism of Christ attributed to the second century, in which John stands on the shore, and our Saviour in a shallow stream, while the Holy Spirit descends as a dove. On the sarcophagus of Junius Bassus, Christ is also symbolically represented as baptized by affusion. The annexed rude example from the Catacomb of Callixtus, probably of the third century, also clearly exhibits the administration of the rite by pouring. It is accompanied by a representation of Peter striking water from the rock,

an emblem, according to De Rossi, of the waters

of baptism sprinkling the sinful souls that come thereto. A similar example also occurs in the cemetery of St. Prætextatus.' (p. 539.)

"Other representations of our Lord's baptism are given in ancient mosaics. Here is one, contained in a church built in A. D. 401 in Cosmedin, at Ravenna. John has a bent rod in one hand and a *patera*, or shell in the other, from which he is pouring water on the Saviour's head. The figure on the left is a mythological representation of the river.

"A still finer work of the same kind is shown in the center piece of the magnificent dome of the Baptistery of Ravenna, dating from A. D. 454. (See the Frontispiece.) Nothing can show more plainly the ancient idea of a river baptism than these paintings.

"In this connection, I will cite certain expressions of the Fathers, showing what these authors regarded as the actual mode of John's baptism. They will serve to throw additional light upon these pictures. Aurelius Prudentius, (born A. D. 348), says, 'He poured water in the river,'—*perfudit fluvio*. Paulinus of Nola (born A. D. 353), remarks, 'He—John—washes away the sins of believers by the waters poured upon them,'—*infusis lymphis*. Lactantius (died about A. D. 330), says, 'Christ received baptism that he might save the Gentiles by baptism, that is, by the pouring of the purifying dew,'—*purifici roris perfusione*. St Bernard, also, speaking of the same event, says, 'The creature pours water upon the head of the Creator,'—*infundit aquam capiti Creatoris creatura*.'[1]

"The next picture, taken from a piece of sculpture at Chigi, near Naples, is believed to be a representation of the baptism of Argilulfus and his wife Theodelinda, king and queen of the Lombards, converted to Christianity in A. D. 591. Mosheim's Ecc. Hist. vol. 2: p. 385.

"I have previously mentioned the baptism of a soldier by Laurentius, the Roman martyr, at

---

[1] Pond on Baptism.

the time of his execution. The view here given of the scene is in the church dedicated to this saint at Rome, extra muros, and represents him as baptizing by pouring in the regular baptistery. The water flows from a jug or vase, of an antique pattern."

"I cannot think," said Joseph, "that any great weight is to be attached to these pictures. They are uncertain both as to date and authorship, and we all know that artists, like poets, use great license in their delineations. Even the renowned Leonardo da Vinci, in his famous fresco of the Last Supper, represents our Lord and his apostles as *sitting* at a table after the modern fashion, instead of reclining on couches, as they undoubtedly did."

"True," said his uncle, "but there is nothing in these pictures, as in that, inconsistent with what we know from other sources were the customs of the times. In this view, we may receive them as a valuable aid in illustrating those customs. It is a remarkable fact, as it seems to me, that in none of these, or any other ancient works of the kind, is there any representation of the *act* of immersion, while nearly all of them do show the act of pouring. What is the proper inference to derive from this fact, I leave for each to decide for himself. The fact, certainly, is eminently suggestive.

"The conclusions, then, to which we are brought as to the opinions and usages of the early church, — say for the first thousand years after Christ, are the following : —

"1. The form of baptism, as a sacrament appointed for and necessary to the salvation of all mankind, must be such as could be administered to all. The fountain of baptism, like that of the water of life, must be made accessible to every one; the adult believer and the infant of a few hours old; the most robust man and the most delicate invalid on the sick or dying bed. Therefore,

"2. Sprinkling and affusion, when necessary, were equally with immersion valid baptism. They answered all the essential ends of the ordinance, and were, if given and received in faith, accepted by Christ.

"3. Infants were baptized as well as adults; indeed, except in the case of conversions from among the heathen, this became the usual and normal way of the growth of the church.

"4. Persons baptized by sprinkling or pouring, whether in infancy or on the sick bed, were not to be rebaptized. Of course, there was no denying to them full communion in the church, or the participation of all the rights and privileges pertaining to any other member.

"5. For ritual reasons, a trine and nude immersion was preferred and made obligatory by church authority, as the regular mode of baptism in all ordinary cases.

"6. A single immersion was, except by a small portion of the western church, regarded as heretical and invalid. Persons who received it were not esteemed as baptized at all, and if they subsequently sought admission to the church, they were received in the same manner as converted heathens, with all the formalities of a full, canonical baptism.

"7. The use of baptismal clothing, full or partial, in the reception of the rite was unknown, and would have been deemed a profanation.

"Here, then, are *seven* particulars involved in the sentiments and practice of the early church, in every one of which the modern Baptists are at variance with them. In four out of the seven, Pedobaptists are in entire agreement with them."

The entire party remained silent for a few moments at the announcement of this result. At length Mary said,

"This is all new to me. I have often heard Baptists boasting that they alone, of all the sects, administer baptism after the example of the early, and for a long time the universal, church; and I supposed it must be so. But surely this does not look like it. They do *immerse*, it is true, but with this sole exception they do not, so far as I can see, follow ancient usage in a single particular; and even this they practice in a way which would have branded them as heretics, and excluded them from the fellowship of all orthodox Christendom. I should like to know, Cousin Joseph, what you have to say to such unwarranted pretensions as this."

"I have nothing to say," he replied, "except that it is charitable to hope that those who make them are not aware of the facts, as your father has now developed them. I confess I was not, for one. I saw in the past that one fact only of immersion, and I thoughtlessly took it for granted that it was just the immersion we now practice, neither more nor less; and as to the other matters related, I either did not know of them or deemed them irrelevant to the subject. I said, at the beginning of the evening, that I feared Uncle Charles would again turn one of our strongest positions against us, and he has done so. For the future I will try to make no claim in behalf of my denomination, which I do not know to be founded in fact."

"A very sensible conclusion," said Mr. Stanley. "Would that we all had the grace to see and acknowledge our errors with equal frankness and sincerity."

Miss Ashton made no remark, but it was not difficult to read in her countenance that she most heartily sympathized in the sentiments just uttered. A solution which she had little expected seemed already about opening for the difficulties which had surrounded her, and she was glad and grateful.

CHAPTER VII.

USAGES OF THE MODERN CHURCH.

"YOU gave us," said Arthur Stanley to his father when they next assembled, "an account of the practices of the early church, in the administration of baptism, down to about the tenth century. I should like, for one, to have the survey extended over the succeeding period to the present time. For, although the existing usages of the church are no certain guide to the interpretation of the Scriptures, still they are valuable as stating what is the *judgment* of Christians generally upon the subject."

"And another thing," said Mary, "will also come into the account, and that is the rise of the Baptists as a distinct denomination. It strikes me that the very fact that they are such, shows that, at the time of their origin, the practice and sentiments of Christendom must have been adverse to their views, else why a separation at all?"

"Such was undoubtedly the case," said Mr. Stanley. "At the time of the Reformation, the Western or Latin Church had generally adopted the simpler mode of administering this rite by affusion. We have seen already that from the first the 'divine compends,' as Cyprian called them, were allowed in cases of sickness or other necessity, and that these were always reckoned, in all the churches East and West, as valid baptism. The minds of men were thus familiarized with this form, and its greater convenience, decency, and healthfulness can not fail to have won for it increasing favor. Strabo, as we have seen, in the sixth century, says, that 'many have been' so baptized, and that it 'usually happens' when the size of the font is disproportioned to that of the person to be baptized. The famous Thomas Aquinas, the 'Angelical Doctor' of the schoolmen, (about A. D. 1255), defended the use of the 'compends' not only as a matter of necessity, but as founded in the New Testament, reasoning, as we are wont to do, that the baptism of the three thousand converts on the day of pentecost must have been in this method. He adds, however, 'It is safer to baptize by immersion, because this is the more common use'. His great contemporary, also, Bonaventura, the 'Seraphic Doctor,' wrote: 'The way of affusion is common in France and other places, and was probably used by the apostles; but the way of dipping is more general.' (Lib. 4. 3. 2.) The Council of Ravenna (A. D. 1311) puts immersion and sprinkling on the same footing. 'Baptism is to be administered by trine aspersion or immersion.'

"The Synod of Angiers, (A. D. 1275), speaks of pouring and dipping as indifferently used, and blames some ignorant priests because they dipped or poured on water but once. The Synod of Lyons in 1287 decreed, 'That danger of baptism may be avoided, let not the head of the child be immersed in water, but let the priest pour water three times upon the head of the child, with a basin or some other clean and decent vessel, still holding the child carefully with his hand'.[1] The Synod of Cambray[2] in 1300, and of Langres[3] 1404, enacted similar rules. The council of Cologne in 1536 say, 'The child is either *dipped*

---

[1] Bib. Rep. vol. 3: p. 373.   [2] Ib.   [3] Miller, p. 96.

or *wetted* with water.' Fifteen years afterwards, in the Agenda of the church of Mentz, published by Sebastian, there is found the following directions: 'Then let the priest take the child on his left arm, and, holding him over the font, let him, with his right hand, three several times take water out of the font, and pour it on the child's head, so that the water may wet its head and shoulders.' Then they give a note to this purpose, that immersion, once or thrice, or pouring of water may be used, and have been used in the church; that this variety does not alter the nature of baptism; and that a man would do ill to break the custom of the church for either of them. But they add it is better, if the church will allow, to use *pouring on* of water. 'For suppose,' say they, 'the priest be old and feeble, or have the palsy in his hands; or the weather be very cold; or the child be very infirm, or too big to be dipped in the font; then it is much fitter to use affusion of the water.' Then they bring the instance of the apostles baptizing three thousand at a time, and the instance of Laurentius, the Roman deacon, and add, 'That, therefore, there may not be one way for the sick, and another for the healthy; one for children, and another for bigger persons; it is better that the administrator of this sacrament do observe the safest way, which is to pour water thrice, unless the custom be to the contrary.'[1]

"The Council of Trent (A. D. 1545–1563) in its catechism enumerates 'three ways of administering baptism,' viz., immersion, affusion, and aspersion, and says, 'Whichever of these rites be observed, we must believe that baptism is rightly administered; for in baptism, water is used to signify the spiritual ablution which it accomplishes. Hence baptism is called by the apostle, *a laver*, (Titus 3 : 5, Eph. 5 : 26) but ablution is not more really accomplished by the immersion of any one in water, which was long observed from the earliest times of the church, than by the effusion thereof, which we now perceive to be the general practice, or aspersion, the manner in which, there is reason to believe, Peter administered baptism, when, on one day, he converted and baptized three thousand persons.'"

"You have remarked," said Joseph Mason, "that this departure from the ancient canonical practice probably arose from an impresssion of the superior convenience, decency, and healthful-

---

[1] Miller pp. 96, 97.

ness of the compendious form. Is there any positive evidence of that fact?"

"Yes, — not in formal statements, perhaps, but in incidental allusions to the subject, which are no less decisive. In a council held in Florence in 1439, a dispute arose between two ecclesiastics, one in behalf of the Greek Church, and the other of the Roman, in which the latter defends his church from the charge of innovation. 'We do not,' says he, 'immerse the infants' heads; for we cannot teach them to hold the breath, nor can we prevent the water from going through their ears, nor can we close their mouths. But we so put them into the font as to omit nothing which is really necessary for the carrying out of the tradition, the laver being a sort of image of the womb, and by this image of the womb setting forth the regeneration. And lest the head, which is the seat of all the senses and the vehicle of the soul, may be without holy baptism, we take up water, in the hollow of the hand, out of the sacred font, and pour it over, etc. For, when a tyrant charged it upon St. Apollonius, as a reproach, that he had not been washed in baptism, and that, therefore, he was not a Christian, God, in kindness, heard the saint's prayers, and satisfied his desires. For a cloud being sent down from above, bathed his head in dew. If, therefore, pouring upon the head be not baptism, it would not have been so done, but in some other way.' (Harduin, Conc. ix. p. 620.) The reason here assigned for pouring is to avoid the danger of suffocating the child, a danger which, in the case of those young and tender, would be very serious, from the trine immersion. A Greek writer of our own day, in a work entitled 'Orthodoxie et Papisme,' thus inveighs against a Catholic author who objected to the former practice: 'It is thus that the notorious apostate, Arcudius, in blaming the baptism, by immersion, of the Orthodox [Greek] Church, terms it offensive, indecent, and abominable, and pushes calumny so far as to accuse the Greek priests of infanticide, asserting that they drown infants.' Dr. Wall, in his History of Infant Baptism, makes the following statement as to the practice of the Church of England. He is speaking of the time of Queen Elizabeth. 'The latitude given in the Liturgy—[referring to the use of the 'compends'], which could have had but little effect in the short time of King Edward's reign, might, during the long reign of this queen, produce an alteration proportionably greater. It being allowed to weak children, though strong enough to be brought to church, to be baptized by affusion, many fond ladies and gentlewomen first, and then, by degrees, the common people would obtain the favor of the priest to have their children pass for weak children, too tender to endure dipping in the water,' especially, as Mr. Walker observes, 'if some instance really were, or were but fancied and framed, of some child's taking cold, or being otherwise prejudiced by its being dipped.' Part 2. ch. 9.

"These citations are sufficient to show the feelings which were extensively entertained on this subject,—feelings which would naturally increase in strength with the general increase of knowledge and refinement, and especially with clearer views of Christianity as a spiritual religion, and of all rites and forms as only symbols of truth, and not saving ordinances of themselves. For why, it would naturally be asked, if pouring and sprinkling are *valid* baptism, as all the church believes, should we cling to immersion, a method, as then practiced, so cumbrous, so dangerous to health, and so offensive to modesty and Christian decorum? These feelings found expression from time to time, as we have seen, in the writings of theologians and ecclesiastics, and the decisions of local councils, until they were finally embodied in the enactments of the Council of Trent, by which sprinkling and pouring, equally with immersion, were fixed as the canonical usage of the Catholic church."

"What were the views of the Reformers on this subject?" inquired Miss Ashton.

"They did not differ essentially from those of the Catholics, but rather, with the clearer light which the Scriptures shed on all outward rites, they were confirmed in the sufficiency of the simpler forms of administration. Luther admitted that the etymological import of the word *baptism* was immersion, but said that that mode had mostly gone out of use, and gave the sanction of his own practice to the other modes. In his translation of the Scriptures, he used the word *taufen* for baptizo, connecting it with *mit wasser*, that is, *with*, not *in* water. In Mark 7: 4, he renders *baptizo* by *waschen* to wash. *Taufen* is used solely of the rite of baptism, which the Lutherans perform by sprinkling. Its signification, as given in the German Lexicons, is, 'To initiate into the church by the sacrament of baptism, to baptize, to christen.'

"Calvin made a similar acknowledgment as to the primary meaning of the word, but held expressly that, as a Christian ordinance, the form of baptism is not essential. 'The difference is of no moment whether he that is baptized be dipped all over, and if so, whether thrice or once, or whether he be only wetted with the water poured on him.' He drew up, also, for the use of his church at Geneva, and afterward published to the world, a form of administering the sacraments, where, when he comes to order the act of baptizing, he words it thus: 'Then the minister pours water upon the infant, saying, "I baptize thee," etc.— Wall. Part 2.

"Turretin says, 'Baptism, viewed as a ceremony, consists in washing, which is done by water, (1 Pet. 3 : 21) either by sprinkling or immersion. As sprinkling is by no means repugnant to the institution of Christ, so it can be shown by examples that the apostolic and primitive church practiced it.' The churches of England and Scotland recognize both modes as proper, but in practice, they perform immersion very rarely."

"Is it not a fact," said Joseph, "that the Westminster Assembly of Divines decided in favor of allowing baptism by sprinkling, by a majority of only one vote?"

"No; it is not a fact. The question as to the mode of baptism was not before the Assembly at all. It was a question as to the 'Directory of Public Worship.' The committee appointed to prepare this had, in their report, used this language, 'It is lawful and sufficient to sprinkle the child.' To this, Dr. Lightfoot and others objected, not because he doubted of the entire sufficiency of sprinkling, for he decidedly preferred it to immersion, but because he thought there was an impropriety in pronouncing that mode *lawful* only, when no one present had any doubts as to its being so, and almost all preferred it. Others seemed to think that by saying nothing about dipping, that mode was meant to be excluded, as not a lawful mode. This they did not wish to pronounce. When, therefore, it was put to the vote, as reported, there were twenty-five votes in favor and twenty-four against it. The real question, therefore, as Dr. Lightfoot himself says, was, ' sprinkling being granted, whether dipping should be tolerated with it.' This vote was afterward reconsidered, and instead of the expression as first reported, the following was adopted: ' He is to baptize the child with water, which, for the manner of doing it, is not only lawful, but sufficient and most expedient to be by pouring or sprinkling of the water on the face of the child, without adding any other ceremony.' "[1]

"The Oriental Churches," said Joseph, "retain, I believe, the ancient practice unchanged."

"The Greek Church does, baptizing by a triple immersion, in a state of nudity, with the ceremonies of exorcism, insufflation, the use of oil, etc. At the same time, the 'compends' in cases of necessity are admitted as valid.

"Mr. Chrystal[2] quotes the testimony of Asseman and Goar, as follows: ' The Greeks generally baptize by *pouring* thrice a large quantity of warm water (by which, according to a canon of a provincial Synod, under Germanus, Archbishop of Amathus, the fervor of baptism is signified,) upon the head. The child sits in a vessel or deep laver, up to its shoulders, while they wash it, or, lest it should be overwhelmed by the abundance of the water, or should drink too much, the priest places it, lying down and sustained

---

[1] Miller p. 120.
[2] History of the Modes of Baptism, p. 165.

by the priest's left hand, upon its stomach, and then he purifies its head and whole body with the saving waters.' Upon this statement Mr. C. observes, ' Now, while it may be doubted whether this remark was true even at the period when made (1749) of the " Orthodox " Greeks in the sense which it conveys, *i. e.* " generally," (plerumque), nevertheless it is clear that *sometimes* the Greeks, even those of Constantinople and the Patriarchates, who are now much stricter in their requirement of trine immersion of Westerns passing to them than the Russians, did at that time receive the Latins or others who had been baptized only by affusion or aspersion, without immersion, and as validly, though it might be irregularly, baptized, and they themselves, in case of necessity, and often perhaps, even when none existed, did use the compends and do even now in that case.'

" ' The whole Greek and Russian communion, for a long time, up to 1756, did receive Western baptism as valid. Since then, the Greeks have rejected it; but it should be remembered that they esteem all not of their own creed as heretics, so that this may have added some little weight with them in their decision, even if a main reason were its lack of trine immersion. Indeed, more or less from the days of Michael Cerularius, in the eleventh century, until 1756, the whole Orthodox church, Greek and Russian, had, at times, admitted Western baptisms performed by the compends and without necessity, as valid. At Florence, (A. D. 1439), Gregory, the Greek monk, rejoins to Mark of Ephesus, that he (Mark), had never seen Latins baptized by Greeks. These facts (and the above remark, so far as it applies) show that, like other parts of the church, they have not always acted regularly and rubrically. Since the period when this was written, the rule in favor of trine immersion has been more insisted upon in the Patriarchates. In Russia, however, which includes the great bulk of this communion, the baptism of Latins, Lutherans, and Calvinists is admitted.'

"Passing further to the East, we find the Armenian Church enjoining both sprinkling and immersion in their mode of baptism. Their ritual directs, — 'He is to place the infant in the font, and is to apply some of the same water with his hand upon its head, and is to say thrice, N. is baptized, &c. But while saying these words the priest shall thrice immerse the candidate, burying thrice in the water the guilt of original sin,' etc.[1]

"The Ritual of the Syrians, at Antioch, prescribes: 'And he shall let down the child into the baptistery, with its face turned toward the East, and shall place his right hand upon its head, and with his left shall take up water, saying, "N. is baptized," etc. And he shall raise it out of the water.'[2]

"The office of the Syrian Church of Jerusalem directs: 'Then shall he let him down into the baptistery, the face of the person to be baptized being turned toward the East, but the priest's toward the West. And the priest shall place his right hand upon the head of the person to be baptized, and shall take up some of the water which is in front of the person to be baptized, with his left hand, and shall pour it on his head. In the same manner, he shall take up some of the water which is behind the candidate, and shall pour it upon his head. Finally, he shall take some of the water from the right and left sides of the candidate, and shall pour it on his head. And he shall wash his whole body. The priest shall not remove his right hand, nor

---

[1] Chrystal p. 122   [2] Ib. p. 123.

shall he place his left hand on the head of the person to be baptized, as ignorant priests do; but his right hand remaining on the head of the child, he shall take up the water with his left, for it is written, John placed his right hand only on the head of our Lord.[1] But when the child has been let down into the laver the priest shall say thus, 'Such a one is baptized,' etc.[2]

"The Ritual of the Syrian Maronites is nearly identical in its directions for the performance of baptism with the one just given.[3] The custom of the Nestorians, also, appears to be the same. When Mar Yohanan, the Nestorian bishop, was in this country in 1842, he stated to Dr. Ducachet of Philadelphia, who relates it, that they baptized children by putting them in the font, in a sitting posture, up to the breast in water, facing the East, and then pouring water on them in the name of the Father, Son and Holy Ghost. He stated also, 'Such is the kind of baptism practiced all over the East at all periods;' also that so universal was the baptism of infants that he had never seen an adult baptized"[4]

---

[1]See this attitude illustrated in the representation of Christ's baptism given on p. 256.

[2]Chrystal, p. 124.   [3]Ib. p. 129.

[4]Hodges " Baptism Tested," p. 389.

"Rev. Mr. Newell, one of our first missionaries to India, visited the Syrian Christians of Malabar, in 1814. He says 'I made particular inquiries respecting the mode of baptism in the Syrian church, I found it was affusion.'[1] This East India church is very ancient. It claims to have been planted by the apostle Thomas, and as early as the fourth century, the missionary, Theophilus, found churches there.[2] Their liturgy and rites were doubtless derived from sources independent of all the churches in the West.

"On the whole, then, it appears that the practice of the Baptists in respect to the mode of baptism, and the treatment of those who adopt a different mode, is as opposed to the usages of the universal church beside, at the present day and for the last eight hundred years, as it was during the thousand preceding years. None of the great historic churches, east or west, sanctions it, none of their sister Protestant denominations agrees with it. By their own act they have cut themselves off from the communion of all Christendom beside. They have carried out to their logical results the declarations of Dr. S. F.

---

[1] Taylor's Ap. Bap. p. 176.
[2] Neander, Ch. Hist. p. 48.

Smith, before quoted, that 'the Baptist church is *the only church of Christ on earth.* It is not a schism, but every other body professing to be a church, is a schism.'"

"Where then, father, was the church of Christ, I should like to know, before the Baptist church originated, some three hundred years ago?" said Mary.

"A question you may well ask," replied her father. "Taking the Baptists' fundamental principles, that only those immersed in adult years are really baptized persons, and that only baptized persons are members of the church and entitled to the Lord's Supper, and we are obliged to say that three and a half centuries ago *there was not a church of Christ on earth*, and had not been for more than a thousand years!"

"Oh, brother Charles, how can you say that!" exclaimed Mrs. Mason. "Christ has always had a church on earth ever since he ascended up to heaven, according to his promise, that the gates of hell should not prevail against it."

"Nevertheless, my statement is true, if Baptists' principles are true. For, certainly, organizations of such only as are now admitted to your churches did not for more than ten centuries exist on earth."

"But," said Joseph, "have there not been in every age some who dissented from the current faith,—heretics they may have been called, yet only because they were such dissenters,—holding essentially the opinions taught by the modern Baptists. They have been known under various names, as Donatists, Novatianists, Paulicians, Cathari, Albigenses, etc."

"Such sects there have been, undoubtedly, but down to the twelfth century there was not one which did not hold to and practice infant baptism. Of course, these were not, on Baptist principles, true churches. I will not now go into the detailed proof of a fact well known to every student of ecclesiastical history. A single statement from the learned Dr. Wall will be sufficient.

"Irenæus, Epiphanius, Philastrius, St Austin, [Augustine] and Theodoret, who wrote each of them catalogues of all the sects and sorts of Christians that they knew or had ever heard of, do none of them mention any that denied infant baptism except those who denied all baptism. They do, indeed, mention some sects that used no baptism at all. St. Austin observes, they were all of them such as disowned the Scripture or a great part thereof. But my meaning is that, of all the sects that owned any water baptism at all, they mention none that denied it to infants.' Then, after rapidly surveying the authors of the following centuries, and especially of those who had written on the heresies of those times, Dr. Wall sums up as follows. 'That I may tell the reader in short the substance of the places to which I have referred him, they do all speak of infant baptism as of a thing taken for granted, and those that do at all enlarge on the matter, do speak of it as absolutely necessary to the infants' obtaining the kingdom of heaven. And this, whether they be of the predestinarian or semipelagian opinion. And I am confident there is no passage in any author, from this time to the year of Christ 1150, or thereabouts, that speaks against it.'"

"At that time, then, it appears," remarked Arthur, "that there was not, according to Baptist principles, a Christian church on earth. Every 'so called church' baptized infants, which was no baptism, and bodies so constituted were still unbaptized persons, and of course no churches. What happened then at that date? Was there a reinstitution of the lost church of

Christ, and a new gift of the sacrament from its divine author?"

"Oh, no. The event referred to, doubtless, was the appearance of a man named Peter de Bruys, an Albigensian, who was the first person, so far as we know, that publicly opposed infant baptism, while retaining adult baptism. The date, however, was a few years earlier than that mentioned by Dr. Wall, say from 1110 to 1130. His followers were called Petrobrussians. They spread throughout Switzerland and Germany, and subdivided into several sects, among whom were the fanatical Anabaptists, who, in the time of Luther, committed such excesses in Germany, and after filling the land with the horrors of rapine and war were finally subdued by force of arms. Of the same source were the Mennonites, a much more respectable body of Christians, who continue to the present day, having a considerable number of churches both in Europe and in our own country. But though these followers of De Bruys discarded infant baptism, there is no evidence that they differed from the Catholic church generally as to the *mode* of baptism, which, as we have before seen, was at this time mostly performed by pouring or sprinkling, as it is universally among the Mennonites at this day.[1]

"So then," said Mary, "after all, the Mennonites had no true churches. Though they baptized adults only, yet as they did not immerse them, it was no valid baptism. Besides, even if it were, how did they get it? Can persons not in the church institute a church? Can those who were never baptized, baptize others?"

"Well, that is a problem for the Baptists to solve, not us. Menno himself expressly affirmed that baptism had been wholly lost. 'Here thou hast,' says he, 'the due custom of baptizing in Christ's church, which *had been obliterated for a very long period, and had perished*, but by the most ample gift of God hath been *restored anew*. He who reads with Christian judgment, and understands well, will wish well to this celestial truth of Christ, which *during so many ages was lost*, but is now discovered, and with good cause will he return great thanks to God,'" etc.[2]

• "Have the Baptists, then, derived their churches and baptism from him?" asked Mary.

"No; though this is sometimes claimed for

---

[1] Chrystal, Mode of Baptism, p. 294.   [2] Ib. p. 301.

them. The Mennonites, as I have said, are not immersionists, and the Baptists have no fellowship with them. 'Baptists disown as their spiritual progenitors,' says Dr. J. M. Peck, 'the Reformers of the 16th century, as they also do the pseudo reformers of modern times.' Ch. Review, 1857, p. 5.

"Where then did they get their church existence, and their baptism? I am curious to know how what had been so long extinct was recovered again. You say there was no new revelation from heaven reinstating it, and the old maxim tells us '*ex nihilo nihil fit*'—out of nothing nothing comes; so I don't see how the lost boon was restored to men."

"We shall see," replied her father, "their own account of it presently. 'The first regular congregation of English Baptists,' says Mosheim, (vol. 3: p. 473), 'appears to have originated from certain English Puritans who returned from Holland after the death of their pastor, Rev. John Smith.' Smith had been an English clergyman, but separating from the Anglican church, he fled to Holland, where, in 1606, he joined Rev. John Robinson's congregation, at Amsterdam. Here he embraced Arminianism, renounced pedobaptism, and, at length, withdrew from the Congregational church, and with some associates formed a new church. Robinson himself relates the event thus. (Works III, p. 168). 'If the church be gathered by baptism, then will Mr. Helwisse's appear to all men to be built upon the sand, considering the baptism it had, and hath, which was, *as I have heard from themselves*, on this manner: Mr. Smith, Mr. Helwisse, and the rest, having utterly dissolved and disclaimed their former church, state, and ministry, came together to erect a new church by baptism... And after some straining of courtesy who should begin, and that of John Baptist, (Matt 3: 15), misalleged, Mr. Smith *baptized first himself*, and next Mr. Helwisse, and so the rest, making their particular confessions.' Smith died in Leyden in 1610, but Helwisse returned to England, and from him the Baptists' views and practice spread more or less through that country.

"'The Particular, or Calvinistic Baptists trace their origin,' says Mosheim, 'to a congregation of Independents established in London in the year 1616. This congregation, having become very large, and some of them differing from the others on the subject of infant baptism, they agreed to divide. Those who disbelieved in infant baptism were regularly dismissed in 1633 and formed into a new church under Rev. John Spilsbury.' Of course the pedobaptist church from which they were dismissed, being 'no church,' they had had neither baptism nor true church membership, and must have created for themselves both, as Smith had done. It has been sometimes said that they sent persons to Holland to procure and bring to them a true baptism, but the statement is without authority, and altogether improbable,[1] for

---

[1] "Crosby (*Hist. Eng. Baptists*, i: 102) and others who have disrelished the notion of deriving the baptismal lineage of their denomination from a man who baptized himself, have sought comfort in a theory that one company of English Baptists sent over 'one Mr Richard Blount, into the Netherlands, who obtained his baptism from some Dutch Baptists there,' and so disseminated through England, and afterwards through this country, a more genuine and respectable article. There are two difficulties here. In the first place, there is no sufficient evidence that any Mr. Blount thus went. All the testimony is of the most fearfully hear-say character. Mr. Hutchinson 'had heard' the story, and this was 'confirmed' by an account given by an anonymous manuscript, 'said' to be 'written by Mr. William Kiffin.' But, granting that he did go, and was thus baptized, there is no proof that his baptism was by immersion; for, as we have seen, the Dutch Baptists of that time were not immersers; the fact being that the Collegiants, as they were called, the followers of the three brothers Van der Codde at Rhysberg about 1630, seem to have separated from the other Dutch Baptists as much on the doctrine of immersion, as on abolishing the office of the ministry, so that their rise appears to mark the date of immersion as the practice of a portion of professing believers in Holland.

"And in the second place, there were plenty of Baptist churches in

Spilsbury himself elaborately argues the power of unbaptized persons to originate baptism for themselves.[1]

"The first Baptists in America were Roger Williams, and the church which he founded at Providence, R. I. Contrary to the popular impression, Williams, at the time of his expulsion from Massachusetts, did not profess to be a Baptist, and therefore was not expelled for being one. His offense was that of assailing the validity of the Massachusetts charter granted by King James I., and 'defaming' the ministers and magistrates of the colony. He appears to have been led to profess Baptist views by a Mrs. Scott who came

---

England long before the date of which Crosby speaks, whose practice as to the mode of baptism was precisely that of the Dutch Mennonites. They opposed infant baptism, but they did not immerse This is abundantly proved by existing documents, and notably by a correspondence carried on by them through a period of years with some of the Dutch Mennonites; and it is fully and honorably conceded by Evans (vol. ii: 52). He says, 'There is positive proof, if credit is to be given to the testimony of men living at the period, that there were communities in existence then, who conformed entirely to the mode adopted by our Dutch brethren.' A writer in *Mercurius Rusticus* (p. 25) says of Chelmsford, England, that the Baptists there practiced both ways: 'the one they call the Old Men, or *Aspersi*, because they were but sprinkled; the other they call the New Men, or the *Immersi*, because they were overwhelmed in their rebaptization.'"

Dr. Dexter, in Congregationalist, Jan. 29, 1874.

[1] See the evidence as to the origin of the Baptist church presented in full in Chrystal's Mode of Baptism, p. 237, seq.

to live in his colony.[1] The 'History of the First Baptist Church at Providence,' says, 'Mr. Williams and those with him considered the importance of gospel union, and were desirous of forming themselves into a church, but met with considerable obstruction. They were convinced of the nature and design of believers' baptism by immersion, but from a variety of circumstances, had hitherto been prevented from submersion. To obtain a suitable administrator was a matter of consequence. At length, the candidates for communion nominated and appointed Ezekiel Holliman, a man of gifts and piety, to baptize Mr. Williams, who, in return, baptized Mr. Holliman and the other ten.' Chrystal, p. 240.

"Such, then, is the answer to your inquiry which the Baptists themselves give as to the origin of the existing church of Christ and its sacraments. It began with John Smith, John Spilsbury, and Roger Williams. All the regular Baptist churches now in existence are derived from them, and according to our modern Dr. Smith, there is no other Christian church on earth."

"Well," said Joseph, "do not all Christian

---

[1] Mass. Hist. Soc. Coll. vi, p. 338.

denominations admit the validity of lay-baptism when required by necessity?"

"But this was not lay-baptism at all. That is simply the administration of the sacrament by a layman, *i. e.*, a private member of the church, in distinction from a minister. But, according to their own account, neither of these persons was even that. Neither was in the church at all. As Menno said, it had been *obliterated*.

"I ought, in justice, to add that this view of the matter is frankly admitted by Baptists themselves, as indeed they are compelled to do by the strictest logical necessity. John Smith, as I have said, argued stoutly for the validity of his self-baptism. 'Now for baptizing a man's self, there is as good warrant as for a man's churching himself; for two men singly are no church, jointly they are a church, and they both of them *put a church upon themselves;* for as both of these persons unchurched yet have power to assume the church, each of them for himself and others in communion, so *each of them unbaptized hath power to assume baptism for himself* and others in communion.' So, too, Crosby, a distinguished Baptist historian says, 'The greatest number of the English Baptists, and the more judicious . . .

affirmed and practiced accordingly, that, after a general corruption of baptism, an unbaptized person might warrantably baptize, and so begin a reformation.' Chrystal, p. 249.

"To all which, we may appropriately reply, in the quaint language addressed to Mr. Smith at the time, by a writer signing himself, 'I. H.,' 'I pray you tell vs one thing, Master *Smith?* By what rule baptised you your selfe? What worde or example had you for that in all the Scriptures? Doe you affirme the baptisme of children to be the marke of the Beast, because, you say, there is no word nor example in all the Scripture, to proue that they may be baptized; And yet durst you presume without either word or example, to baptize your selfe? If you go about to proue that lawful which you haue done, by any word, or example in the Scripture, I say you cannot set one step forward to that purpose, but you must allow thereby the baptisme of Children. I marvell you did not preuent this objection: which wil be as hard a bone for you to gnaw vpon as you thinke the baptisme of Children is to vs. It was wonder you wold not recieue your baptisme first, from some one of the Elders of the Dutch Anabaptists: but you will be holyer then all, and see how you haue marred all.'

"There is another remarkable thing about Smith's self-baptism, that ought not to be omitted. All the facts connected with it go to show that *even this was performed by sprinkling or affusion!* 'This,' says Dr. H. M. Dexter, 'was the manner usual at that time among the Baptists of Holland. Frederick Müller, a Baptist of Amsterdam, and one of the most learned men, in some directions, now living in Holland, says: "Neither the Waterlanders, nor any other of the various parties of the Netherlands' *Doopsgezinden* [Baptists], practiced at any time baptism by immersion." (Evans's *Early English Baptists*, i: 223.) So that if Smith had started out with any new theory of the *mode* of baptism, it becomes inevitable, first, that he would have alluded to, and defended it, in some one of his own controversial works and various efforts at self-defense; and, secondly, that some, at least, passing reference should have been made to it by the various writers of the time, who discussed him and his career.'

"Smith subsequently was convinced that his proceedings were unlawful, and a little before his death, he made an acknowledgement of his error, in a work entitled ' *The last Booke of John Smyth:*

called the Retractation of his Errours, and the Confirmation of the Truth.' In this he says, 'I did never acknowledge yet, that it was lawful for private persons to baptise, when ther were true churches and ministers from whence wee might have our baptisme without synne; as ther are 40 witnesses that can testifie: onlie this is It which I held, that *seeing ther was no church to whome we could Joyne with a good conscience to have baptisme from them, therfor wee might baptize ourselves.*' — Congregationalist, March 5, 1874.

"Such, then, is the baptism and the church origination upon which that denomination stands to-day, and from which, in boastful self-confidence, it pronounces all other churches a 'schism' and a 'slab.' Such is the rite urged upon us, in place of that which has been held to be valid in every other church that has existed, from the apostolic age to our own. Against such a claim, argument, surely, is useless. If the bare statement is not enough to refute it, nay, to show its amazing assumption, no reasoning could do so. Let the instincts of an enlightened Christian understanding, and a generous Christian heart, judge of it."

CHAPTER VIII.

THE RATIONAL ARGUMENT.

"THIS must be our last evening of discussion, I think," said Mr. Stanley, when they next met. "You must all be weary of it, by this time, and, in reality, there is not much more that I care to say on the subject."

"Oh, no, uncle, not weary of it," said Joseph, "I assure you. It has been a very interesting discussion to me, and I hope as profitable as interesting."

"So we all say, I am sure," added Mary. "I should be sorry to leave it, till the whole argument is presented. You have not taken up the subject of close communion yet, and I should like to see what can be said, pro and con, respecting that. It is a very practical subject for you, Cousin Joseph, and is likely soon to be still more so," she added, with a significant glance at Nellie.

"Oh, that is simply a matter of inference from the main facts established. If, as Uncle Charles has nearly convinced me, immersion is not taught in the Bible, it cannot be insisted on as one of the terms of communion. Still, I should very much like to hear what he has to advance on that subject."

"We will proceed then," said Mr. Stanley, "to the only other topics necessary to complete our discussion. Hitherto, we have surveyed what I may call the Scriptural, the Classic, and the Historical Arguments. It remains only to present some general considerations growing out of the nature of Christianity, which perhaps may be designated the *rational* argument. Nor is this an improper argument even in the case of a positive institution of the Bible, for it is one which both our Lord and his apostles employed. 'How think ye?' he often asked of his hearers. 'Why, even of yourselves, judge ye not what is right?' 'I speak unto wise men,' said Paul, 'judge ye what I say.' 'Prove all things; hold fast that which is good.'"

"And you know," remarked Arthur, "that the

thing we proposed in the outset was to take 'a common sense view' of the subject."

"My first remark then is, that, considering the nature of Christianity as a revealed system of grace and salvation for mankind, it is reasonable to assume that its great initiatory rite would be such a one as would be *practicable for all*. Immersion, in my view, is not such a one."

"I suppose you refer to the difficulty of applying it to the sick and infirm, — the ancient *clinici*," said Joseph.

"Yes; but not to them exclusively. There are many conditions of human life and experience, in which immersion, as a rule, could not be employed. There are desert lands where water itself is scarce. Dr. Coan, the veteran missionary at the Sandwich Islands, says, 'A large portion of the island of Hawaii is entirely destitute of streams, or considerable fountains of water. I have often been called to administer baptism to the blind, to the lame, to the very aged, to believers upon their death-beds, where there was no body of water within ten, twenty, sometimes thirty miles, large enough to permit the immersion of the head, much less the whole person. Many of these believing candidates could not have been removed to a distant fountain except at the cost of life. In every place, however, where I found man, I found a little water, often only that which had been collected, drop by drop, in caves of the mountains; and with these precious drops I sprinkled their bodies, as their hearts had been already "sprinkled from an evil conscience" with the infinitely more precious drops of the Saviour's blood.'

"There are climates, also, of such severity that open streams or pools are rarely accessible. In Greenland, Lapland, and Siberia, the rivers and lakes, in the winter, freeze to the bottom, and no water can be had except by melting snow and ice. There are seasons of the year, in all countries except those within the torrid zone, in which the rite cannot safely be administered. It is true that, in large and wealthy churches, baptisteries are constructed, where warmed water may be used, but this cannot be done generally."

"But, Brother Charles, you know that people are baptized, in the open air, at all seasons, and with perfect safety," said Mrs. Mason.

"I know it has often been done, and that persons have often, though not always, apparently escaped any evil consequences from it. But this does not affect the truth of my proposition in general. Dr. Hall (p. 115) mentions a baptism which took place in the winter in the Delaware River, when a hole was cut in the ice, in which sixty men and women were immersed, the weather being so cold that a number of men were employed in stirring the water with poles to keep it from freezing while the immersion was going on."

"That reminds me," said Arthur, "of what I read in the New York Tribune not long since. Its correspondent, writing from the Adirondack region, protested against the terrible exposures there incurred by immersions, following a revival during the winter. 'On bitter cold days,' says he, 'with the thermometer at zero, the rough rivers, hid in thick ice, are bared with axe and spade, and the converts,—often young girls of tender age, are plunged in. As we see them struggling in evident fear and agony, shrinking from their water-soaked garments which freeze about them, we can but ask if *this* be imitating the blessed Master. Had Christ preached and baptized in this climate, would he who healed the sick have risked the life of the body to purge out the stains of girlhood? It is one of the inexpressible inconsistencies of weak humanity, that followers of the Divine Lord should in his name commit cruelties that unbelievers would shrink from.'"

"I agree in those sentiments," said Mr. Stanley. "The laws of life and health can no more be violated under the plea of obeying Christ, than the law of the ten commandments. It is no less a presumptuous tempting of God, than Christ's leaping from the pinnacle of the temple would have been, under the solicitations of the devil.

"But this argument holds with special force in relation to the sick and infirm. We have seen how the common sense and Christian feeling of the early churches revolted against the bondage of ritualism in their day. And such must be the dictates of the Christian instinct in all ages. Invalids, persons of delicate constitution, the sick, and the dying, make together a large aggregate who at all times need, and are specially entitled to, the consolations of the gospel and its ordinances. It is to them emphatically that the gospel comes as good news, with its precious assurances of the Saviour's sympathy and love. Are such to be told when they desire to receive the appointed tokens of that love, that they do well to desire it, and doing this they have discharged all their duty, and must be content with that; that *because* they are too weak to receive them, and beyond even the strong need the strength to be derived from them, therefore they must not have them? Is this all the grace which the gospel, as represented in the Baptist church, has for the sick and dying?

"'I once,' says a ministerial friend, 'had the joy of ministering to such a soul in the last days of her earthly life. She was a young woman cut down by that scourge of our climate, consumption. I had, in repeated visits, told her of Christ and his salvation, and had the delight of seeing her rejoicing in his love. A little before she died, she expressed a wish to join the church and receive the sacraments he had appointed. Her request was granted. As she could not leave her bed, the church appointed two of its members to go with the pastor and receive her in its name. We assembled in her room on a summer Sabbath afternoon. She lay propped upon her pillow, her hollow cheek, save for its hectic flush, rivaling the sheet in whiteness, while her bright eyes beamed with celestial hope and peace. I read and received her assent to the articles of faith and the covenant, then, dipping my hand in water brought in a white bowl, I applied it to her brow in the name of the Father, the Son, and the Holy Ghost, in token of the higher baptism of the Spirit which we believed she had received, and sealing her to Christ and to his people forever. Then, breaking the sacramental bread and pouring the wine, we knelt around the bed and showed forth the Lord's death in sweet and grateful remembrance of him. Could I, as a minister of his, have refused the delightful service to which I was thus called, and coldly have told that dying child that the grace of baptism was not for her, because, forsooth, she could not go and be plunged into the waters of the neighboring river?'

"No, Christ has never appointed for mankind a rite which the most needy, for whom it was appointed, cannot receive. To insist upon it is to dishonor the gospel itself; to bind heavy burdens and grievous to be borne, and most heavy upon the feeblest and least able to bear them."[1]

---

[1] The late General Rawlins, Secretary of War, expressed in his last moments a strong desire to be baptized. He *was* baptized on his death-bed in the only way it could be done, and professed his faith in Christ. Ought he to have been denied this privilege because he was unable to be immersed?

"It is no wonder, I think," said Mary, "that Baptists often speak of baptism as a *cross to be borne*, and exhort young converts to take up their cross, and follow Jesus into the water!"

"I have here a poem," said Nellie, "which I recently cut from a Baptist paper, expressive of this idea."

MY BAPTISM.

"I stood beside the *dreaded* waters brink
    And saw a grave;
I looked to heaven, and rays of purest light
    Gilded each wave.

I thought of persecution's sneer and frown,
    The world's proud scorn,
Then raised my eyes to Him who bore for me
    Earth's crown of thorn.

Beneath the sacred waters, solemnly
    I bowed my head,
And found a couch sweeter and softer far
    Than downy bed.

'This *heavy cross*, dear Lord, I bear alone
    For Thee,' I said,
And lo! the cross a crown of glory shone
    Upon my head."

"This view of baptism, as a cross to be borne, is a very common one among our Baptist friends, yet it is wholly unscriptural. Where in all the New Testament is such an idea conjoined with this beautiful ordinance? No man and no church has a right to make a cross of that which Christ himself hath not made one. As well put on sackcloth, or scourge yourself with whips, or wear pebbles in your shoes, and call it service to the Lord. Do we not hear him asking in indignant rebuke, 'When ye come to appear before me, who hath required *this* at your hand?'

"And this brings me to my second remark under this head. It is contrary to the whole tenor of Christianity as a spiritual religion, to exalt any mere outward rite to the importance which is claimed for the mode of baptism. Herein Christianity is in direct contrast with the ancient law. That prescribed rites and forms. It dealt with men as children who could not walk alone. It told them not only what to do, but how to do it. The tabernacle and all its furniture, even to the pins which held its curtains; the dress of the priests, with the tints of its embroidery, and the graving of its jewels; the victims to be sacrificed, and the treatment of every part, whether 'baked in the oven,' or dressed in the frying pan, or 'with cakes mingled with oil;' the utensils for the service from the altars and the laver, to the tongs, and the snuffers; the material and the mode of every thing were minutely prescribed. No deviation in any point was allowed. Mode and form were essential. But after almost two thousand years of such schooling, it was assumed that the time had come for mankind to be *men*. The gospel, accordingly, looks at *things* not forms. When under the force of the old education, or through the natural obtuseness of the heart, men clung still to the shadow more than the substance, it taught them to disregard form altogether. Oh, how the Pharisees stood aghast when Jesus trampled under his feet their cherished ritualisms — not washing his hands before eating; not keeping the Sabbath after their fashion; eating and drinking with publicans and sinners, and most heinous of all, declaring that Jerusalem was not the sole place in which to worship God! So, too, how Paul cut the knot of their endless contentions about circumcision, and meats, and new moons, and Sabbaths, and fast days. 'Be not' said he, 'in bondage to such things. Leave the first principles and go on unto perfection. Let every man be fully persuaded in his own mind. For meat destroy not thy brother. For neither if ye eat are ye the better, neither if ye eat not are ye the worse. The kingdom of God is not meat and drink, but righteousness, and peace, and joy in the Holy Ghost.'

"Such is the spirit of Christianity, free, gracious, expansive, as the very love from whose infinite bosom it proceeded. And yet, we are told, there is one exception. There is one rite enjoined upon all men, to be performed in just one invariable way, a way which multitudes of men cannot obey, and yet so essential that without it no obedience is rendered; and standing, as it does, at the door of the church, the church itself cannot otherwise be entered; so that no immersion, no baptism; no baptism, no church; no church, no covenanted title to the kingdom of heaven!"

"But our brethren do not reason thus in respect to the other sacrament," observed Arthur.

"No, I will do them the justice to say they are, in this, happily inconsistent with themselves. Yet, if ritualism were to be allowed to usurp either, it might do it with much the greater plausibility in this case. 'Do *this*,' said our Lord, 'in remembrance of me.' Now we know much more of the way in which the Supper was first observed, than the first baptism administered. We know that it was in an upper room, at night, while they were reclining on couches, no females being present. We know that the loaf which Jesus took into his hands to break was unleavened bread, and that the cup was the unfermented passover wine, — leaven, whether of meat or drink, being strictly forbidden in that solemn festival. (Ex. 13: 7.) Why, then, do they not insist that we must exactly imitate all these things when we come to the table of the Lord? Nay, more, with the exception of John and Andrew, (John 1: 35, 40), there is not a shadow of evidence that one of the twelve, then present, had ever been baptized at all, while there is an absolute certainty that not one of them had received Christian baptism, for it had not then been instituted. Why do they not insist as strenuously on form here, as in the other case, and appeal as confidently to the express words of Christ, 'Do THIS'? And I answer, because their own good sense revolts from it. They know that none of these things can affect the spiritual significance or value of the rite; that the Lord can be obeyed, and true communion with him and his people enjoyed in it, if only the heart be right, however much, or however little conformity be had to the precise mode of that first supper in the upper room at Jerusalem."

"It has often seemed to me," said Mary, "that if the mode of baptism had been intended to be so essential, the command would have been given so plainly as not to admit of an honest mistake."

"I think so too," said her father. "And this was what I designed to say in my third remark."

"But we Baptists contend that it has been made such," said Joseph. "Our teachers tell us that the word *baptizo* has such force, so that the command itself, in its own terms, is explicit and unmistakable, by all sincere inquirers after truth."

"And yet, they must admit that it has been mistaken, if doubt as to the alleged force of that word be a mistake. All Christendom, except the Baptists, by their own showing, have mistaken it, which is only the same thing as to say that the command was not given in the way we may presume it would have been, if the alleged strictness of obedience in letter and form were required. On this point, let me commend to you the judicious remarks of the late Archbishop

Whately, in relation to what he calls, 'Omissions' in the Scriptures. His idea is, that these omissions show that the inspired writers were supernaturally withheld from recording whatever, in word or act, was not meant to be authoritative over all mankind.

"'We seek in vain there,' says he, 'for many things which, humanly speaking, we should have most surely calculated on finding. No such thing is to be found in our Scriptures as a catechism, or regular elementary introduction to the Christian religion ; nor do they furnish us with any thing of the nature of a systematic creed, set of articles, confession of faith, or by whatever other name one may designate a regular, complete compendium of Christian doctrines ; nor again do they supply us with a liturgy for ordinary public worship, or *with forms for administering the sacraments*, or for conferring holy orders ; nor do they even give any precise *directions* as to these and other ecclesiastical matters — anything that at all corresponds to a rubric or set of canons.

"'Now these omissions present a complete moral demonstration that the apostles and their followers must have been *supernaturally withheld* from recording a great part of the institutions.

instructions, and regulations which must, in point of fact, have proceeded from them; withheld *on purpose* that other churches, in other ages and regions, might not be led to consider themselves bound to adhere to several formularies, customs, and rules, that were of local and temporary appointment; but might be left to their own discretion in matters in which it seemed best to divine wisdom that they should be so left."[1]

"These remarks are eminently sensible, and must commend themselves to the judgment of all thinking men. Indeed, we may affirm, as with the force of an axiom, that what was essential to the existence of the church must have been declared so plainly that mistake concerning it should be impossible."

"I cannot resist that conclusion," said Joseph. "That, surely, would be no revelation from God, which did not reveal what was essential to the very ends for which a revelation was given."

"From the word of God, then," said Mr. Stanley, "let us turn to his providence. If the rejection of immersion be an error so great as to vitiate one of the sacraments, and even extin-

---

[1] Kingdom of Christ, p. 77. Also Appendix D. p. 258.

guish the church itself, (for we are told that there is no church on earth but the Baptist church) then it were reasonable to say that *God's blessing could not rest upon those who practiced such error.* 'This,' says Dr. Smith, 'was Christ's imperative command,' and 'an apostle would have said, if a man refuse exact obedience to Christ, he is none of Christ's.' Now we know that God heareth not sinners; of course he will withhold his Spirit from those who are thus willfully disobedient. But is it so? Has he not owned the ministry of Calvin, Owen, Baxter, Wesley, Whitfield, Scott, Griffin, Alexander, Nettleton, Kirk, and the hosts of the non-immersed who have preached his gospel in all lands, and in all the centuries since his ascension? Has he not given his Spirit to render the word preached by them effectual to the conversion of multitudes? Have not many, inspired by his love, gone to the heathen, and, in self-forgetting fidelity to him, proclaimed the news of salvation, and organized the converts granted to them into churches? Were not these his ministers? Would he have so signally honored their work if they were not?

"And where can be found more lovely exhibitions of the spirit of Christ than among those who belong to these churches? Are not those who have been baptized by sprinkling or pouring, as holy, as spiritual, as exemplary in life and conversation, as those who have been immersed? Are they not as prayerful, as self-denying, as fruitful in all good works and all Christian enterprises? Have they not as much of the spirit of missions, and are they not as liberal in sustaining those whom they have sent forth? If the test which the apostle applies to himself in writing to the Corinthians be the true one, ' The seal of my apostleship are *ye* in the Lord,' then are these ministers the ministers of Christ, and these churches are his churches."

"Of course we acknowledge the piety and benevolence of Christians of other denominations," said Mrs. Mason. "We think they are in error as to baptism, but we do not pretend that it is an error fatal to piety itself or inconsistent with the enjoyment of God's blessing."

" Yet little short of this is implied in the language of Dr. Smith. 'An apostle would have said, if a man refuse exact obedience to Christ,' — and he means in reference to this matter, — 'he is *none of Christ's.*' What more could he say of a profane man or an infidel?

"And this brings us to the only remaining consideration which I wish now to adduce, and that is the unhappy practical consequences which flow from the position and sentiments of our Baptist brethren.

"These consequences are manifold. It pains me greatly to refer to them, yet justice to our subject forbids that they should be wholly omitted."

"I hope, uncle, you will speak freely just what you think," said Joseph. "We are all friends here, and shall not be hurt, for we know that while you would not 'extenuate,' neither would you 'set down aught in malice.'"

"I should hope not," replied Mr. Stanley. "Let me, then, mention first the ill-effect of this doctrine upon those who hold it. I will not dwell upon the needless inconveniences and even hardships to which they subject themselves, in endeavoring to carry out what they think to be commanded by the Lord, — the 'crosses' they make out of it, fatal sometimes even to health and life. I cannot think their position favorable to the best state of mind and heart. It tends to awaken a self-complacency, not to say a self-conceit, which is any thing but 'lovely and of good report.' Prof. Stuart, in his great article on the Mode of Baptism, published in the Am. Bib. Repository, gives, as one of the reasons why he was induced to write it, the reception of a letter from a correspondent, of which the following is an extract: —

"' As those who are not immersed but adopt a form of man's invention do not obey the Saviour's command, so they will not, all other things being equal, *enjoy the highest seat in heaven.* Regeneration is the only qualification necessary to *enter* there. All who have been born again will see God. But in heaven there are different grades of happiness. The degree which each will enjoy will be proportioned to the fidelity of his obedience. To explain more fully my meaning : — of two persons, who have in every other respect thought and acted and spoken alike, but the one was *immersed* and obeyed, while the other was *sprinkled* and did not obey, *the former must have a higher place in heaven than the latter.* If then he would be as happy as possible in heaven, ought not he who believes immersion only to be baptism to practice it? Nothing is more common than to hear persons say that the observance of the form is not essential. If they mean it is not essential to enter heaven, we grant it. But to enjoy the most happiness there, it is essential, since we cannot obey unless we do it.'"

"I hope you do not hold the entire denomination answerable for such foolish utterances as that," said Mrs. Mason.

"Certainly not; it is too marked an exhibition of spiritual vanity to do aught but excite disgust in all who behold it. And yet, that such is the legitimate *tendency* of those views, — for the error of this writer is not so much in his reasoning as in his premises, — seems very evident, and may I hope be said without any breach of charity."

"But however that may be, there can be no question that it does tend to censoriousness and uncharitableness toward other Christians. Recur again to the language of Dr. S. F. Smith in the article already cited. (p. 11) Here we are unchurched outright, without an if or but. And there are other things in that article no less offensive even to Christian courtesy. 'What then,' he asks, 'are we to think of the prayer in the Litany of the English Church, repeated every day for hundreds of years, "From all heresy and schism, good Lord, deliver us." Has

God allowed so many devout men for these many years to offer this petition to the Answerer of prayer, and yet to pray in vain? I reply, *They have no right to expect God to answer such a prayer.* Let *them* answer it by returning to the bosom of the true church,'—(*i. e.* the church of John Smith and John Spilsbury, which was not originated till centuries after the Litany was composed). 'God has given his inspired word to them as to us, which is sufficient to guide them into all truth. They do not need a fresh revelation, or a fresh exercise of divine power to save them from heresy (Greek, *hairesis,* difference) and schism. The plain word of God translated by themselves is all that is needed by them. Let them follow it meekly, reverently, cheerfully, and exactly, and then, and not till then the prayer, "From all heresy and schism, good Lord, deliver us," will be answered.'

"I cite these words of Dr. Smith, because of his eminence among Baptists, and his beautiful hymns delight many Christians of other denominations than his own. Sad indeed is it that we should be compelled to associate with his name other words breathing a spirit so different from theirs.

"Here is another similar utterance from the Rev. George B. Taylor, Editor of the Christian Review for April 1858, one of the standard publications of the denomination. It is from an article entitled, 'Qualifications for the Lord's Supper.' 'If the question were whether we are to recognize an unbaptized [*i. e.* unimmersed] man as officially qualified to preach and administer the ordinance, we could not hesitate to answer in the negative. . . . We cannot regard him as any more entitled to preach than any other unordained man of similar gifts. . . . If this unbaptized brother desires to occupy our pulpit, and have the use of our meeting-house and the ear of our congregation, we are free to say that while he has no absolute claim for these things, Christian courtesy and regard for truth and the common cause should incline us cheerfully to grant them. Nor should we in all this recognize this unbaptized Christian brother *as a member, much less as an officer, of a visible church.*'"

"Indeed, father," said Mary, "how very grateful you ought to be for such professions of 'Christian courtesy,' from one whose own sacramental lineage boasts so august an origin as the self-baptism of John Smith or the mutual immersion of Roger Williams and Ezekiel Holliman!"

THE RATIONAL ARGUMENT. 319

"I trust, my dear, I am suitably so. But the subject is not a pleasant one to dwell upon, and I gladly pass it by. I should not, however, forbear to quote the declarations of the American and Foreign Bible Society, supported by the Baptists, in their Annual Report for 1840.

"'Resolved — that the nations of the earth must now look to *the Baptist denomination alone* for faithful translations of the Word of God.' And referring to the refusal of the British and Foreign Bible Society and the American Bible Society, to yield to their demand that the word *baptizo* and its derivatives shall be translated by terms equivalent to immerse, etc, in versions prepared for use in heathen lands, they charge these venerable institutions with 'virtually *combining to obscure* at least part of the divine Revelation, and to circulate versions of the Bible *unfaithful*, at least so far as the subject of baptism is concerned.'

"But the worst of all the evils connected with the claims of our Baptist brethren, are the unscriptural doctrine and practice of *close communion*."

"Our practice is not peculiar in this, as has very often been proved," rejoined Mrs. Mason.

"Our communion is no more close than yours, for you do not admit those whom you regard as unbaptized persons to the Lord's table."

"We do not invite any that are not *Christians*, but we exclude none that are. If we did, it would only show that our practice is as contrary to the spirit of the gospel as yours. And if there are any who are thus exclusive in fact, let them share in the same condemnation. But it is not so. The terms of admission to church membership are one thing, to the Lord's Supper quite another. Your own Dr. Olmstead, of the Watchman and Reflector, in his recent communion with Christians of other denominations in London, has vindicated the act on what I accept as the true ground. The Supper does not belong to the church, but to all believers. It was instituted and first celebrated before there was a Christian church, and the first communicants, as I have before said were, a majority of them, unbaptized persons.[1] We invite to it all, therefore, who give evidence of piety. We mention no names, we specify no sects, we do not refuse any who profess to be the Lord's and desire a place at his table. Even if a pious Friend who discards all

---

[1] See Robert Hall's Terms of Communion. Part 1. Section 2.

baptism, like Gurney, or Mrs. Fry, or our sweet singer, Whittier, should propose to sit down with us there, we would not say him nay. We hold that it is the Lord's table, not ours; and that all have a right to it whom He invites, not we.[1]

"Close communion has no warrant in the Word of God. Dr. Smith says, 'We have not a direction or permission in the whole New Testament for an unbaptized person to celebrate the communion, nor a clear example wherein any unbaptized person did so. Can you present one?' I ask him in turn, when was Simon Peter baptized, or James, or Philip, or Bartholomew, or Thomas, or Matthew the publican, or James the son of Alpheus, or Thaddeus, or Simon the Canaanite? And yet they participated in the first communion. He may say they had been baptized by John. But how does he know this? Not a hint of the kind is upon record. Even if they were, it was not *Christian* baptism. 'My deliberate opinion,' says Robert Hall, 'is that in the Christian sense of the term they were not

---

[1] It is related of the venerable Father Sewall, of Maine, that being present once at a sacramental occasion in a Baptist church, he was passed by in the distribution of the bread and the wine. After the rest had partaken and he plate and cup were returned to the table, the good old man stepped forward and helped himself to the sacred emblems, saying, as he did so, 'This brethren, is *the Lord's table* and I have as good a right to it as any of you.'"

baptized at all. From the total silence of Scripture, and from other circumstances which might be adduced, it is difficult to suppose they submitted to that rite after the Saviour's resurrection; and previous to it, it has been sufficiently proved that it was not in force.' (Works I. p. 303). The claim that they had been baptized is a pure assumption, and yet necessarily, it is a corner stone to the whole system of close communion. For if our Lord himself communed with unbaptized persons, then his followers may.

"On the other hand, the New Testament expressly commands believers not to let their speculative differences be a bar to Christian fellowship. 'Him that is weak in the faith receive ye, but not to doubtful disputations. Who art thou that judgest another man's servant? To his own master he standeth or falleth; yea, he shall be holden up: for God is able to make him stand. Wherefore receive ye one another, as Christ also received us to the glory of God.' (Rom 14: 1–5; 15: 7).

"Close communion has no support in the practice of the universal church till within very recent times. The early churches rejected *heretics*, impure in life or corrupters of Christian doctrine, but none whom they believed to be true disciples of the Lord. In particular, they never made baptism, either as respects mode or subjects, unless conjoined with heretical doctrine, an occasion of non-communion. Says Mr. Hall again, 'They (close communionists) are the only persons in the world of whom we have either heard or read who contend for the exclusion of genuine Christians from the Lord's table; who ever attempted to distinguish them into two classes, such as are entitled to commemorate their Saviour's death and such as are excluded from that privilege. In what page of the voluminous records of the church is such a distinction to be traced? Or what intimation shall we find in Scripture of an intention to create such an invidious disparity among the members of the same body? Did it ever enter the conception of any but Baptists that a right to the sign could be separated from the thing signified; or that there could be a description of persons interested in all the blessings of the Christian covenant, yet not entitled to partake of its sacraments and seals?'[1]

---

[1] See the masterly argument of Rev. Robert Hall for open communion in his Works Vol. 1. pp. 283, 504.

"It is well known that the vast majority of English Baptists are followers of the views of Mr. Hall. Never have I enjoyed the sacramental service more than on the occasion when I was permitted to join in it with Mr. Spurgeon's church in London, and he gave us his right hand welcoming us most cordially to the table of the Lord. We felt that the service was a showing forth of the Lord's death, not of the divisions and follies of his people.[1]

"Close communion exerts the most baleful influence upon the peace of families. A Christian wife has prayed for years for her impenitent husband. She has held up before him her own pure

---

[1] Even in this country close communion has not always been the rule. The fundamental article in the covenant of the first Baptist church ever gathered in Massachusetts — that formed at Swansea in 1663 — declares that:

"Union to Christ is the sole ground of the communion of Christians, and so they were ready to accept of, receive to, and hold church-communion with, all such as in a judgment of charity, are fellow members in the Head Christ Jesus, *though differing in such controversial points as are not absolutely and essentially necessary to salvation.*" (*R. I. Hist. Coll.* iv: 20.)

" Here is an old Baptist opinion as to what constitutes liberty of conscience, by a body of men who knew whereof they affirmed; who had been in their own persons and households persecuted for righteousness' sake; and written by one who had — before his persecution — been of a different judgment All honor to John Myles and his little company, for so noble a testimony, so nobly uttered." Dr. Dexter.

example, and has besought him with the tenderest entreaties to turn to the Saviour. At last God hears her prayer, and the voice of joy and praise ascends from the newly erected altar of that household. And now, twice married in the holiest ties, she would bring her husband with her to the communion table. But a Baptist minister has persuaded him that immersion alone is baptism, and has succeeded in drawing him into the water. 'No, madam,' he tells her, ' you cannot sit down with him at Christ's table. Only on one condition may the longing of your heart be gratified. Renounce your own baptism; tell the world that the faith of your parents when they brought you in infancy to the sacred font was a superstition; turn your back upon them, and on all those with whom you have hitherto walked in the Lord; go into the water, and then you may come and commune with your husband!' A father and mother wrestle with the angel of the covenant in prayer for the conversion of their children. Their prayers are answered, and one after another they are brought to Christ. But, alas, when they would welcome them to the fold of the church, they find that they have imbibed from some source the opinion that immersion is essential and close communion a duty. And so the unity of the family is broken, and instead of walking to the house of God in company they go different ways, and the parents sit childless at the sacramental feast.

"Not long since, a lady who had been many years absent in missionary service, returned with her husband to this country on a visit to her home and friends. Consecrated to God in infancy by her pious parents, and blessed with faithful Christian nurture, she early became a disciple of the Lord. Subsequently, she espoused the views of the Baptists, and went forth as a missionary among the heathen. On this visit to her native land, as the time drew near for her return, her venerable father expressed a strong desire that ere she left, to meet him no more probably on earth, he might have the comfort of sitting with her again at the table of the Lord. But no : — *he* was unimmersed, and the longing of his heart was denied! Was that a sacrifice, we ask, on the part of either, which Christ required? And will that missionary wish to tell the story to the converts from heathenism among whom she labors, to show unto them the kindly spirit of the gospel she has brought them?

THE RATIONAL ARGUMENT. 327

"How unhappy the feelings which this unchristian practice awakens among Christians of different names! 'Woe to the world,' said Christ, 'because of offenses. It must needs be that offenses come, but woe to that man by whom the offense cometh.' Much more may we add, Woe to that evil *thing* by whom it cometh. Such claims, and such judgments of others, as close communion implies *are* offenses of the gravest character. We do not, I hope, resent them; and certainly, we have no wish to obtrude ourselves upon the fellowship of others when we are not wanted. But we lament these things for *their* sakes, and for the sake of the common name of Christians which we wear."

"Why, then," said Mrs. Mason, "do you not, yourselves, remove the obstacles to that fellowship? You acknowledge that immersion is baptism, and that all modes are alike valid. Why not, then, adopt *our* mode, and all difficulties will vanish in a moment."

"For all the reasons that I have now, at so great length, exhibited. While we admit that immersion is baptism, we do not believe that it is the only mode, or the Scriptural mode, or the most fitting mode. Besides, to yield to it, would, for us, be to sanction an unreasonable ritualism, which imposes unwarranted burdens on tender consciences, and makes crosses out of what should be a delight. We should feel ourselves violating all those commands that bid us look beyond forms to the substance; to worship God in the spirit, and rejoice in Christ Jesus, and have no confidence in the flesh. No; much as we desire unity, there is a price at which even that must not be purchased. We cannot give up the precious birthright of our sonship, the liberty wherewith Christ hath made us free.

"And it is not alone to them and other denominations, that close communion is a cause of evil; it is a leaven of mischief among Baptists themselves. Here is an article taken recently from the 'Baptist Union,' the names only being suppressed. I know not whether the statement be true or not, but if it be, or even if it be possible, ought it not to stamp with everlasting reprobation such a disturber of the peace in Israel?

"'Rev. ——— has recently asserted in public, that an arrangement has been made by a few ministers, by which they can prevent any liberal, [*i. e.*, open-communionist] minister from securing a pastorate, and that he had defeated the settlement of —— over the —— church, though nearly the whole church desired his services.

"'He also mentioned Messrs. ——, ——, ——, ——, and —— by name, and said that, while it might be impossible to unsettle them, they could and would prevent them from securing any new pastorates. He spoke particularly of Dr ——, as now desiring a church, and said that he would be defeated in every effort to secure one, unless he emphatically retracted his liberal utterances, and pledged future loyalty to close communion. We are assured that the action of the —— church has been dictated by this influence.'"

"And does it need any argument to show that a practice, of which these are the direct fruits, must be a serious hindrance to the progress of Christ's cause? Do we not know how often worldly men point to it, and to the contentions caused by it, as proofs that Christians are no better than they? Says a ministerial brother, — 'When a young pastor, I welcomed to my pulpit, one Sabbath morning, an Agent of the Sunday-School cause. Eloquently did he advocate it, as a *union* work, dwelling on the good it was effecting in the frontier settlements of the West, because it ignored sectarianism, and brought all

Christians to labor together for the salvation of the young. My church responded liberally to his appeal; and at the close of the service, we remained to celebrate the sacramental supper, it being our regular communion day. I invited the brother to stay and assist me in the services, but, with an embarrassed manner, he excused himself on the ground that he was a Baptist, and withdrew. Of what worth were all those beautiful appeals for *union* in Christ's work, followed by such an example as this?'

"I have, myself, had the privilege of laboring, as a missionary, on heathen ground; and you, my children, were born there. I can speak of the tendencies of sectarianism upon the people of those lands. For the most part, I am glad to say, that missionaries of different denominations withhold the exhibition of their speculative differences from the observation of the heathen; nay, that the work of saving souls, which absorbs their hearts, obliterates, to a great extent, those differences themselves. No more delightful examples of Christian union are to be found, the world over, than may be seen among the brethren of different names, on many of the mission-fields of the East. And I do not hesitate to affirm that, were it otherwise, — were the churches gathered from amidst the heathen to practice the same exclusiveness and sectarianism which too often prevails here, it would be a more formidable hinderance to the success of the gospel than caste, and polygamy, and all the social vices that prevail among themselves. For these can be made to fall before the power of the truth wielded by the Spirit of God, but those destroy the power of the truth itself.[1]

---

[1] The following facts are stated on the authority of Rev. Horatio Bardwell, late of Oxford, Mass., and formerly a missionary of the A. B. C. F. M. in India.

"When the second band of missionaries whom the American Board sent to India, arrived in that country, they were uncertain for a while where their place of destination would be. In the mean time, they abode with a Baptist missionary of England, who had been laboring for many years, and had not seen the face of an English or American Christian. He received them with open arms, invited them to preach, and extended to them all the hospitality within his power. By and by a communion season came. Our missionaries not wishing to set their Baptist brother on the defensive by entering into an argument, merely tried the force of an appeal to his conscience. They went into the church in a body, and seated themselves in a remote part of the house, by which it was known that they did not expect to commune. The native converts, never having heard of close communion, were astounded. 'What!' said they, 'these Christian ministers, whom we have been taught to love and recognize as Christians, retire from the Lord's table!' The Baptist missionary kept weeping all the while he was administering the elements to the people, but said nothing. As he came out of the house, he advanced to our missionaries, and taking them by the hand, gave vent to his feelings in a flood of tears. In the midst of uncontrollable sobs he exclaimed, 'Brethren, I do not believe the Lord ever meant to try his people so.' 'No,' said the mis-

"And if there was needed one word more to exorcise this evil spirit of sectarianism, we may surely find it in the love of Christ to us all, and his last prayer to his Father that we all may be one. It may be that we cannot all interpret the Scriptures alike, nor agree precisely as to the modes of baptism, of worship, of ordination; that we cannot always adopt the same methods of Christian work; but can we not love as brethren? Can we not yield to each other the privilege of acting according to the light that is given to us, and even receive those whom we think 'weak in the faith?' Can we not, *ought* we not, to meet at the table that bears the memorials of our common salvation? Partaking of the same viands has been regarded, in every age and among all nations, the proof and the pledge of friendship. Can we not give each other this token?

---

sionaries, 'it is a trial of your own making.' 'Well,' said he, 'I will go home and think of it.' The result was that he renounced close communion, and afterwards sat down in consistency with his Christian conscience at the table of the Lord with his brethren. And so kind was he that, though he retained his other Baptist sentiments, he allowed the American missionaries to baptize one of their infants in his own chapel." New Englander, vol. xiii; p. 579.

The above incident I have heard Bro. Spaulding speak of. The minister's name was Chater, of Columbo, where the missionary band — Spaulding, Winslow, Scudder, and Woodward, — landed. H.

"There is a melancholy cadence running through all our memories of the late Alliance, when we think that there could be no response to Christ's loving command, 'Do this in remembrance of me;'— when we think of those dear Christian brethren who had come thousands of miles to demonstrate the unity of his people, but were not permitted to eat and drink at his appointed feast together.

> "Ah woe! ah grief!
> Beyond belief!
> Oh, could you not e'en once agree
> When you were met to talk of Me?"

"Political parties forget their strifes around the grave of a buried chieftain. Sundered families bury their differences, and clasp the hand of forgiveness when the death of a parent melts them in a common sorrow. And shall not the memorial supper of our dying Lord, if no other scene may, be permitted to testify that his people are one? Will they not there, if no where else, cease their controversies, suspend their censorious judgments, and let the hearts which really are kindred with each other in the unity of Christ's love, reveal that kinship in the unity of their own?

"A few years ago, a company of travelers from England and America were spending the Sabbath together in Jerusalem. It was, if I mistake not, at the passover season, and, with a common impulse, they met for worship in the 'Cœnaculum,' or upper room, still shown as that in which the last supper was held. The scene and its associations suggested the service which should follow, and it was spontaneously agreed to spread anew, in that place, the memorials of the Saviour's dying love. There were ministers and members of several different denominations present. As the sacred service was about to begin, one of the party, a Baptist, and, I think, one or two more arose and left. All that remained sat silent under the suggestions thus awakened. At length, Dr. C——, also a Baptist, but one who had learned to love his Lord more than his sect, arose, and drawing nigh to the table said, with a voice tremulous with emotion, 'Can *I* turn my back on these memorials of my Lord, because some of you are of a different Christian household from myself? I am a Baptist, but I hope I am more,— a Christian. Methinks I see the look of our dying Saviour turned to me with sadness and love, as if to say, "Will ye also go away?" And let my answer to-day be, "Lord, to whom shall I go? For where thou art, there is my abiding place; thy table is my table; and all those that love thee, and meet there to testify that love are my brethren."'

"May the time speedily come when this noble sentiment shall find a response in all Christian hearts; and wherever the Lord's table is spread, and loving disciples gather about it to show forth his death till he come, may each one say, 'Where Jesus is, there is my place; and all they who meet each other there in faith and love are MY BRETHREN.'"

SYNOPTICAL INDEX.

	PAGE
PREFACE.	3
CONTENTS.	7
THE EVANGELICAL ALLIANCE.	9
Exhibition of Christian unity.	10
A Communion season desired.	11
Objected to by Baptists.	11
Mrs. Mason and her family.	12
The Stanleys.	13
Close Communion.	13
Baptists only in the Church of Christ.	14
Assertions of Dr. S. F. Smith.	14
Exclusiveness of Baptist views.	17
The charge retorted on other denominations.	18
A discussion agreed upon.	20

I. THE SCRIPTURAL ARGUMENT.

THE BAPTISMAL COMMISSION.	24
How to determine its meaning.	24
Illustration from Blackstone's Commentaries.	25
How did the Apostles understand it?	26
I. WHAT MEANS they had of understanding it.	26
1. They were familiar with *John's baptism*.	27
a. Reasons for believing this was not immersion.	27
(1.) The great multitudes baptized.	28
Populousness of the country at that time.	28

Meaning of the word "all."	29
Did John stand in the river?	30
Did he have assistants?	31
(2.) The want of baptismal garments	32
(3.) No proof from his baptizing in Jordan	35
The wilderness was his home	33
Abundant water needed for other purposes	34
(4.) No proof from the words "into" and "out of."	35
b. Reasons for believing it was done by sprinkling	38
(1.) The example of Moses at Mt. Sinai.	38
(2.) The law of purification required sprinkling	39
John's baptism not regarded as new	39
Personal immersions not enjoined	40
His baptism termed a purifying	43
The prediction of a Purifier by Malachi	44
(3.) It was a symbol of the baptism of the Spirit	46
Remark. Christ's baptism not our example	49
Either in its nature	49
Or in its design	51
c. John's baptizing at Ænon.	53
Locality of Ænon.	54
Meaning of "much water."	54
This needed for other purposes than immersion.	54
2. They were familiar with the baptism of *proselytes*	58
Evidence that it was then practiced	58
The mode of it	60
Special reason for this	61
Value of Rabbinic testimony	63
3. They were familiar with the *teachings of the Old Testament.*	66
a. Sprinkling always the rite of purification	66
b. Sprinkling was to characterize the new dispensation	67
c. Old Testament examples of baptism.	69
(1.) Naaman the Syrian leper	69
(2.) Nebuchadnezzar.	71
(3.) Isaiah, baptized by iniquity	73
(4.) Judith.	73
(5.) One who had touched a dead body	78
4. They were familiar with *contemporary usage*	80
a. Baptism before eating	80
Ancient methods of ablution	82
Abyssinian custom	84
Was it the washing of articles purchased?	84
Present Oriental customs	86

  b. Baptism of pots, cups, etc............................. 87
  c. Baptism of tables. 88
    Baptist objections and explanations.................... 90
 5. They were familiar with *Christ's use of the word*........... 93
  a. His own baptism of suffering........................... 93
    Dr. Dale's explanation. (Note.)........................ 95
  b. The promised baptism of the Holy Spirit. 96
    Mode of its fulfillment at the pentecost................ 97
    Verbal expressions used in describing it............... 97
    Meaning of the Greek word *en*......................... 99
    Was this a literal baptism?............................ 100
    Meaning of baptism with fire. 101

II. How THE APOSTLES DID understand the Commission....... 104
 1. As shown from *their own practice*........................... 105
  a. The baptism of 3000 at the pentecost..................... 105
    Time, place, etc. 105
    The time and place of the assembling. 105
    (1.) There was no place for immersing. 106
    Cisterns, pools, streams............................... 106
    (2.) No preparation for clothing....................... 108
    (3.) No sufficient time................................ 109
    Baptismal scene at the Sandwich Islands. 110
    Alleged baptism by Chrysostom.......................... 111
    Alleged baptism by Remigius............................ 112
  b. The baptism of the Eunuch............................... 113
    The supposed locality. 113
    Meaning of "into" and "out of."........................ 114
    Present mode of bathing in India....................... 115
    What suggested baptism to the Eunuch. 116
  c. The baptism of Saul of Tarsus........................... 118
  d. The baptism of Cornelius................................ 120
  e. The baptism of Lydia and her household.................. 122
  f. The baptism of the jailer at Philippi. 124
 2. As shown from *their teachings*.............................. 129
  a. The little prominence they gave to the rite.............. 129
  b. Burial with Christ in baptism............................ 130
    Importance of the phrase in Baptist estimation. 130
    Other figures also used to denote baptism.............. 132
    No outward form can correspond to all these............ 134
    Immersion not like the burial of Christ................ 134
    Source of the figure not in form but in signification... 136
    Baptism never made a symbol of death................... 137

Baptism the symbol of purification.................... 137
Impropriety of the phrase " the liquid grave.".......... 139
The outward rite not a burial with Christ. 140
  c. Baptism of the Jews unto Moses. 142
  d. Baptism of Christians by one Spirit...................... 144
  e. Oneness of baptism. Eph. 4:5........................... 145
  f. Baptism typified by the deluge........................... 146
  g. The divers baptisms of the law........................... 149
  h. The witness of the water. 153
Results of the Scripture argument............................ 158

II. THE PHILOLOGICAL ARGUMENT.

Nature of this argument.. 159
Classic usage no law to Christianity. 159
New Testament Greek peculiar................................. 160
Historical view of it... 160
Illustrations of its peculiarities............................... 162
    Anecdote from Dr. Hall. (Note.). 162
Testimony of Dr. George Campbell........................... 164
Testimony of Ernesti. 165
Testimony of Prof. Stuart...................................... 165
Testimony of Prof. Whittemore................................ 166

  I. CLASSICAL OR PAGAN USAGE............................ 167
  1. Definitions of the Lexicons................................ 168
  2. The word BAPTO. 172
    a. Its primary meaning, to dip............................ 172
    b. Its secondary meaning, to dye, to smear. 172
      The secondary sense formerly denied.................... 173
      The secondary sense as literal as the primary............ 174
  3. The word BAPTIZO. 175
    Distinction between general and specific words........... 175
    a. Its primary meanings................................. 176
    (1.) Does not signify to dip............................. 176
    (2.) Does not signify to plunge.......................... 180
    (3.) It signifies to immerse............................. 180
      But immerse not a modal word. 181
      Examples of eight different modes of immersion. 182
    b. Its secondary meanings.............................. 185
      Denoting effects without reference to modes............ 185
    (1.) Baptism with a drug............................... 186
    (2.) Baptism by wine................................... 187
    (3.) Baptism with taxes. 187

SYNOPTICAL INDEX.   341

   (4.) Baptism with disease............................... 187
   (5.) Baptism with grief. 188
   (6.) Baptism by misfortunes............................ 188
   (7.) Baptism by questions. 188
   (8.) Baptism by excessive labors....................... 188
   (9.) Baptism with sleep. 189
  (10.) Various other baptisms........................... 189

II. USAGE OF THE CHRISTIAN FATHERS......................... 191
  1. Baptism of Elijah's altar on Mt. Carmel. 192
  2. Baptism symbolized by the brazen laver.............. 193
  3. Baptism administered on a couch..................... 193
  4. Baptism by sprinkling. 194
  5. Baptism by pouring.................................. 194
  6. Baptism by circumcision............................. 195
  7. Baptism by Christ's death........................... 195
  8. Baptism by a sword.................................. 196
  9. Baptism by fire..................................... 196
 10. Baptism by martyrdom................................ 197
 11. Baptism by tears. 197
 12. Baptism by crossing the Jordan. 198
    Claims of Baptists compared with these usages. 202

III. THE EARLY VERSIONS OF THE SCRIPTURES.................. 205
  1. Baptismal terms in the Syrian versions. 206
  2. Baptismal terms in the Arabic versions. 210
  3. Baptismal terms in the Persic version............... 210
  4. Baptismal terms in the Egyptian versions............ 210
  5. Baptismal terms in the Latin versions............... 210
  6. Baptismal terms in the Gothic versions.............. 211
  7. Baptismal terms in the Slavonic versions............ 211
    Why these terms were transferred, and not translated..... 212

III. THE HISTORICAL ARGUMENT.

I. THE USAGES OF THE EARLY CHURCH.......................... 214
   Nature of the argument. 215
   Their usages not authority. 215
   Estimate of their value as testimony.................. 215
  1. *In the first two Centuries* the mode not recorded........... 217
   Silence of the Apostolical Fathers.................... 217
   Inferences from this silence.......................... 218
   Testimonies of Justin Martyr and Tertullian........... 219
  2. *After the second Century* immersion was practiced.......... 221

342   THE MODE OF BAPTISM.

  a. It originated in the belief of baptismal regeneration...... 222
    Testimony of Tertullian. 223
    Testimony of Basil of Cæsarea......................... 225
    Testimony of Jerome.................................. 225
  b. Its form was triple, or trine............................... 226
    Believed to be required by the word "baptizo.".......... 226
    And by the form of the commission.................... 227
    Single immersion of heretical origin.................... 228
    Was forbidden by the Apostolic Canons................ 229
    And by a decree of the II^d Ecumenical Council. 230
    The practice of it permitted in Spain, and why. 231
    Was always regarded with disfavor. 232
  c. It was required to be received naked..................... 234
    Testimony of Chrysostom, Ambrose, and Cyril......... 234
    Of Robinson and Wall................................. 235
    Appointment of deaconesses........................... 236
    Remarks of Dr. Miller. 236
  d. Other superstitious ceremonies connected with it. 237
  e. Administered to infants as well as adults................. 239
    Proofs from the Fathers. 240
    Infant baptism no "relic of popery."................... 241
 3. *Sprinkling and affusion allowed when necessary*............. 242
  Immersion often dangerous or impossible. 243
  Decision of Cyprian and the Council of Carthage........... 244
  Clinic baptism... 246
  Distinction between regularity and validity................. 248
  The rule of necessity a liberal one. 250
    Admitted when there was a scarcity of water........... 250
    Admitted in cases of imprisonment. 250
    Admitted when baptistery was small................... 251
 4. *Pictorial representations of baptism*........................ 252
  From the Roman Catacombs................................ 252
  The Font of St. Prisca...................................... 254
  The Font of St. Pontianus.................................. 255
  Other representations. 257

II. USAGES OF THE MODERN CHURCH. 265
 1. Of the *Western or Latin Church*. 266
  Testimonies of Aquinas and Bonaventura. 266
  The Council of Ravenna.................................... 267
  Synods of Angiers, Lyons, etc............................... 267
  Councils of Cologne, Mentz, and Trent...................... 267
  Reasons for the disuse of immersion. 269

    2. Of the *Reformed Churches*.................................... 273
        Luther, Calvin, and Turretin............................... 273
        English and Scotch Churches............................... 274
        The Westminster Assembly.................................. 274
    3. Of the *Eastern Churches*..................................... 276
        The Greek Church. 276
        The Armenian Church...................................... 278
        The Syrian Church... 279
            Statement of Mar Yohanan............................. 280
    4. Of the *Baptist Churches*..................................... 281
        Were the Church and its sacraments extinct?............... 282
        The Petrobrussians and Mennonites........................ 285
        Origin of the denomination................................ 287
            a. The self-baptism of John Smith....................... 287
            b. The baptism of John Spilsbury....................... 288
            c. The baptism of Roger Williams....................... 290
        Smith's defense of self-baptism............................ 292
        His baptism probably by sprinkling........................ 294
        His retractation. 294

IV. THE RATIONAL ARGUMENT.

  I. The rite should be practicable for all...................... 298
        In desert lands.. 298
        In all climates and seasons................................ 299
            Instances of immersion in winter....................... 300
        For the sick and infirm................................... 301
            The dying girl. 302
        No warrant for making baptism a cross................... 304
 II. Christianity does not exalt outward rites................. 305
III. If mode were essential, it would have been defined........ 309
        Whately on "Omissions" in the Scriptures............. 310
IV. Unimmersed churches share God's blessing. 311
 V. Unhappy tendencies of Baptist views. 314
    1. Fostering self-complacency. 314
        A Baptist's letter to Prof. Stuart. 315
    2. Leading to censoriousness and uncharitableness............ 316
        Language of Dr. S. F. Smith.............................. 316
        Language of Dr. George B. Taylor......................... 318
        Language of American and Foreign Bible Society.......... 319

  3. Resulting in Close Communion............................ 319
   This not chargeable upon Pedobaptists...................... 320
     Anecdote of " Father Sewall." (Note.)............... 321
    1. Close Communion without warrant in the Bible. 321
     Unbaptized persons at the first communion............. 321
     Divisions and Separations forbidden. 322
    2. Has no support in history. 322
    3. Is destructive to the peace of families................... 324
     The returned missionary................................. 326
     Why Pedobaptists can not be immersed................ 327
    4. Is an element of contention among Baptists............. 328
    5. Is a reproach to the cause of Christ...................... 329
     The Sunday School agent................................ 329
     The early missionaries in India. 331

VI. Motives to union from the love of Christ................... 332
   The Communion season at Jerusalem...................... 334

www.ingramcontent.com/pod-product-compliance
Lightning Source LLC
Chambersburg PA
CBHW030309240426
43673CB00040B/1112